Historiography and the British Marxist Historians

Socialist History 8

Edited by Willie Thompson, David Parker, Mike Waite and David Morgan

Pluto Press
LONDON • EAST HAVEN, CT

Editorial Team
Willie Thompson
David Parker
Mike Waite
David Morgan

Editorial Advisers
Noreen Branston
Rodney Hilton
Monty Johnstone
Victor Kiernan
Pat Thane
David Howell
Eric Hobsbawm

Published 1995 by Pluto Press
345 Archway Road
London N6 5AA
and 140 Commerce Street
East Haven, CT 06512, USA

Copyright © Socialist History Society 1995

The right of the contributors to be identified as the authors of this work has been asserted by them in accordance with the Copyright, Designs and Patents Act 1988

British Library Cataloguing in Publication Data
A catalogue record for this book is available from the British Library

ISBN 0 7453 0812 0
ISSN 0969-4331

Designed and produced for Pluto Press by
Chase Production Services, Chipping Norton, OX7 5QR
Typeset from disk by Stanford DTP Services, Milton Keynes
Printed in the EC by Watkiss Studios

CONTENTS

Editorial
Willie Thompson — 5

The Road to 1956
John Callaghan — 13

Walthamstow, Little Gidding and Middlesbrough: Edward Thompson, Adult Education and Literature
Andy Croft — 22

Towards a Biography of E.P. Thompson
Harvey J. Kaye — 49

Eric Hobsbawm: A Historian Living through History (Radio Interview) — 54

Raymond Williams: Culture and History
Steve Woodhams — 61

Reviews

Theatres of Memory by Raphael Samuel
Victor Kiernan — 74

Heart of the Heartless World: Essays in Cultural Resistance in Memory of Margot Heinemann edited by David Margolies and Maroula Joannou
David Morgan — 77

William Morris: A Life for Our Time by Fiona MacCarthy
David Morgan — 78

Harry Pollitt by Kevin Morgan and *Rajani Palme Dutt* by John Callaghan
Noreen Branson — 80

Nikolai Bukharin: Bibliographie edited by Wladislaw Hedeler
Francis King — 85

Trotsky as Alternative by Ernest Mandel
Alan Johnson — 87

Compilations of Antonio Gramsci's writings
Mike Waite — 91

CONTENTS

Becoming a Woman and Other Essays in Nineteenth and Twentieth Century Feminist History by Sally Alexander
Christine Collette   94

Creative Meaning: A Book About Culture and Democracy edited by Jerry Rothwell
David Grove   97

Poetry of the Second World War: An International Anthology edited by Desmond Graham
Charles Hobday   98

Women Talk? A Social History of 'Gossip' in Working-Class Neighbourhoods 1880–1960 by Melanie Tebbutt
Karen Triggs   101

Underground Humour in Nazi Germany 1933–1945 by F.K.M. Hillenbrand
Jo Brand   103

Autobiographical writings
M.W.   106

Books Received   108
Information for Subscribers   110
Reports   113
Index   127

The Journal of the Socialist History Society

1. A BOURGEOIS REVOLUTION
1993, ISBN 0 7453 0805 8

2. WHAT WAS COMMUNISM?
1993, ISBN 0 7453 0806 6

3. WHAT WAS COMMUNISM? II
1993, ISBN 0 7453 0807 4

4. THE LABOUR PARTY SINCE 1945
1994, ISBN 0 7453 0808 2

5. THE LEFT AND CULTURE
1994, ISBN 0 7453 0809 0

6. THE PERSONAL AND THE POLITICAL
1994, ISBN 0 7453 0810 4

7. FIGHTING THE GOOD FIGHT?
1995, ISBN 0 7453 1061 3

EDITORIAL

> But I want to argue, first, that the historiography which emerged from [the CP Historians' Group] decisively reworked our notion of the past (so much so that for many today it now appears conventionally mainstream). ...
>
> Bill Schwartz, 'The People in History: the Communist Party Historian's Group 1946–56' in *Making Histories*, 1982.

HISTORY[1] IS AN EVER-POPULAR subject in publishers' catalogues. Although far less numerous, there is also a steady output of texts examining historiography – the enterprise of historical writing.

Every literate culture has practised historiography in one form or another – and preliterate cultures as well, in the guise of myth and oral tradition. However the sort embodied in annals, chronicles and lists of monarchs is generally regarded as a fairly lowly form of historiography. What is taken to distinguish historiography as a form of scientific pursuit (or history from story) is the search for *explanation* – which may of course be, and often is, embedded in a narrative framework. Historical writing in this sense began to be practised roughly two and a half thousand years ago. The advantages of the scientific revolution were certainly not essential for producing historical writing of the highest calibre. The Western intellectual tradition is familiar in the writings of Herodotus and Thucidides, but there exist equally impressive products of Chinese historiography as far back as the beginning of the Christian era, and Arabic examples from the time of the European Middle Ages. Even Dark Age Europe witnessed a first-rank historian, the monk Bede – the first person to systematically use the anno domini convention of dating and who was capable in his historical composition of setting aside the superstitions which permeated the mental climate of the time.

The eighteenth-century Enlightenment saw the beginning of attempts to discern in the human story a theme of progression through stages of development – from 'barbarism' to 'civil society', to use the idiom of the time – one that was related to technical advance, enhanced production methods and improvement in social organisation. It was among certain luminaries of the Scottish Enlightenment, such as William Robertson and Adam Smith, that ideas of this kind first received extended expression, though the eighteenth-century culmination was probably the Marquis de Condorcet, a Girondin revolutionary, whose *Historical Outline of the Progress of the Human Spirit*, which he wrote in the shadow of the guillotine, expressed fervent confidence in a world transformed for the better by linked scientific, social and moral progress.

The idea of historical progression through phases of development towards a future that would in some sense transcend history was central, in a somewhat mystical fashion, to the philosophy of Hegel and, more famously, adopted and adapted to materialist conclusions by Marx. The central assumptions of these approaches however were radically challenged by what was to become the accepted understanding of scientific historical practice.

❑ Ranke and his influence

The principal architect of that transformation was the German Leopold von Ranke (1795–1886). Ranke's revolution in historical studies occurred at a number of levels, both technical and conceptual. He pioneered the study of history as a university discipline, stressed and publicised remorselessly the central necessity of working only from contemporary documentation in any area of study and evolved a critical apparatus for testing the reliability and authenticity of the records in question. No less critical was his abhorrence of indulgence in historical speculation, which he dismissed in favour of the absolute requirement of referencing and citing evidence for every conclusion reached.

But he was also the proponent of the notion of the past as 'another country', the presumption that former ages can only be understood and judged (if they are to be judged at all) in relation to their own times and their own values. The point is an important one. It is perhaps understandable that medieval or Renaissance artists should depict biblical scenes in the costume of their own times, but the anachronistic portraiture reflected the lack of a deeper perception of the historical distance between different eras. Even the great historians of the eighteenth century were not completely exempt from this shortcoming. For all his virtues and insights, Gibbon's Roman senators are still essentially English Whigs in togas. Ranke, on the contrary, maintained – and this was his literal belief – that all ages, though different, are equal in the sight of God. We should not waste time evaluating past eras to see how they measure up against our own, let alone against our hopes for future ones. This standpoint, it is easy to see, involved a total rejection of any progressive view of historical development and implied, moreover, that institutions inherited from a very different past – monarchy or aristocracy for example – might not be simply so much social garbage, manufactured out of superstition and credulity, but possess their own validity.

Indeed there is no doubt that Ranke's deep intentions were counter-revolutionary ones and (he was fairly explicit about this) that he saw his historical principles in such a light. In politics he was a hard-line reactionary and a pensioner of the Prussian monarchy, and was referred to disparagingly by Marx in his correspondence. Schemes of historical development were rejected not only because there was supposedly no good evidence to sustain them but also because they had inspired, and were continuing to inspire, revolutionary endeavours.

Nonetheless, such were the technical merits of his historiography that in the course of the nineteenth century it came to dominate not merely the German academic profession but university-based historical study in all the major states; and no matter how its more extravagant philosophical dogmas may be repudiated its basic insights remain incorporated into all serious historiography down to the present and for the foreseeable future. Like many other traditions it degenerated in the hands of its less imaginative or competent practitioners into an abstracted pursuit of ill-digested historical data on increasingly trivialised themes. Moreover, the important philosophical insight that inhabitants of the past are radically different from ourselves and not simply the raw material of our own much better present can all too easily lead to a perception of them as having no more substance than fictional characters, forgetting that these 'cultural aliens' were real human beings who, in one important respect, exactly resembled those of the late twentieth century – each possessed a life as valuable to its owner as ours are to us. The past is another country – but not a different planet.

❑ Marxist historiography

There is a degree of paradox in the fact that for an outlook so rooted in history, Marxism before the middle of the twentieth century did not, with one exception, produce any really outstanding historiographical tradition. Following the death of its founders many interesting and even significant polemics, observations and reflections, were published,[2] but little sustained enquiry into historically remote eras. The exception was to be found in France, in the field of French Revolutionary studies. It was inaugurated by Jean Jaures who, in the early twentieth century, combined the position of a leading socialist politician with that of a historian of the first rank, with an outstanding historiographical school emerging from his initial work.[3]

The atmosphere of the Comintern and encroaching Stalinism were scarcely conducive to a flourishing historiography of any sort, whether Marxist or of any other kind. It is perhaps worth noting that it was Stalin's letter to a Soviet historical journal, declaring abusively that certain well-known historical facts about Lenin could not be recognised as such, which signalled the end of the relative cultural liberalism in the USSR of the 1920s. The two most significant Marxist historians of the interwar years were – not accidentally – individuals who were forcibly removed from either active political participation or academic study, marginalised and persecuted. Gramsci did not write technical history, but everything he did write, particularly the 'Prison Notebooks', is saturated with a profound historical understanding. Trotsky's *History of the Russian Revolution* remains a classic of the genre: it is contemporary history, written by a leading participant. In both cases the major impact of these texts was to be a posthumous one.

❏ The Historians' Group

The origins and development of the CP Historians' Group have been examined from both within and outside the Group.[4] The starting points were two seminal texts of very different character. The earlier was A.L. Morton's magnificent and erudite popularisation, *A People's History of England*, which can be viewed as an outcome of the Communist Party's Popular Front orientation and subsequent determination to reclaim English history for the progressive movement. The second was Maurice Dobb's very technical (though enthralling) examination of the historical antecedents of British capitalism, *Studies in the Development of Capitalism*, published in 1944. These provided, as it were, the matrix for an interpretation of British history in which the specific studies of the Group's members were framed. All accounts agree that the driving force behind the Group was Dona Torr, an organiser, translator and editor of exceptional calibre, who, tragically, wrote all too little herself of the history for which she was eminently qualified.

The Group as such was formed in the immediate postwar years, during the days of hope in the aftermath of the anti-fascist victory and the election of a majority Labour government in Britain – a time when the USSR was still a respected wartime ally and the CP had two Members of Parliament. Eric Hobsbawm's account conveys vividly the atmosphere of intellectual excitement and discovery in which it conducted its discussions. The Party also had collectives for scientists and writers. These did not long outlast the onset of the Cold War, but the Historians' Group did, and it continued to flourish even though exposed to the academic pressures and persecutions which the Cold War brought in its train.[5]

John Saville has remarked, very perceptively, that the reason almost certainly lay with Soviet behaviour. The CPSU had very definite lines on literature and the arts, as expressed by Zhdanov, Stalin's leading apparatchik in that field; and on science, as exemplified by the notorious Lysenko. The dogmas associated with these individuals and promulgated by Stalin, were imposed on every communist party, creating intolerable strains among their artists and scientists, especially the independently-minded ones, who were trying to relate their professional abilities to their communist beliefs. The Soviet authorities were not concerned however with issuing dogmatic pronouncements on pre-1920 British history[6] and so its historians were left to get on with their business.

Britain at the time was also home to a Marxist historian of the most impressive achievement, in the person of Isaac Deutscher. With his background however, there could be no contact between his work and that of the the Stalinist party. Deutscher's political career had also begun as a communist, albeit a dissident one, in the underground Polish CP. Later he was a dissident Trotskyist and, finally, an individual thinker who had deeply absorbed the cultural heritage of European history and the revolutionary culture stemming from the Russian Revolution. His magisterial biography of Stalin was published as early as 1949, and his even more monumental three-volume study of Trotsky was beginning to appear when the course of events brought about the intersection of his concerns with the politics, if not the professional activities, of the Historians' Group members.

❑ 1956 and after

The catalyst was Khrushchev's denunciation of Stalin's record in February 1956 and the invasion of Hungary by Soviet forces at the end of the same year. The turmoil provoked by these events was not merely mirrored in the Historians' Group, but some of its members emerged as the leading oppositional force within the British party. Edward Thompson and John Saville initiated the intellectual and political debate, Christopher Hill was among the principal spokespeople for the dissident minority at the 1957 Special Congress.

The Group was disrupted. Some resigned from the party or omitted to renew their membership. These included Thompson and, naturally, John Saville and Christopher Hill, who had been at the forefront of the political dispute. Royden Harrison, Rodney Hilton, Victor Kiernan, George Rudé, Raphael Samuel and Dorothy Thompson also resigned. Among those who remained were Maurice Dobb, A.L. Morton and Eric Hobsbawm, although the latter had publicly stated his reservations. Being historians (although, unlike Deutscher, none was a twentieth-century specialist) they could not avoid, in the light of what had occurred, having to confront the historical legacy of Stalinism, evaluate the positive and the negative in the communist experience and reassess the relevance of Marxism as a mode of historical analysis.

Whether or not they stayed with the Communist Party however, all who continued to publish historical research remained Marxist historians, and to their number we must add a further major figure who had been in the British CP. Raymond Williams is generally thought of as a cultural critic rather than a historian, but the two texts which made his name, *Culture and Society* and *The Long Revolution* are clearly historical in their scope. In terms of their historical approach they remain united by a humane undogmatic Marxist approach, with many individual variations and modulations.

❏ The historiographical tradition

Forty years on it is possible to assess the importance of the tradition which emerged from the crisis of 1956, and the quote at the head of this editorial is even further reinforced 13 years after it was written. Central to the tradition's significance is the concept of 'history from below' – but not in any antiquarian or sentimental sense: it is never forgotten that the anonymous masses to whom these historians began to give a voice are part of an evolving historical process with its own internal logic. Edward Thompson's remark on 'the enormous condescension of posterity' has rightly gone around the world and this tradition began the process of rescuing from that condescension the groups he named and many others like them.

EDITORIAL

Thompson is certainly the member of the Group whose name is most familiar to the general public. His monumental and classic work incorporated all the themes which the Historians' group had addressed – class formation and popular struggle, the endless resourcefulness and patience of the masses and the malevolence of the state – but also the possibility of forcing the latter to respond to popular demands. It was also written in passionate opposition to the apologists for two forms of heartless social engineering – Stalinist industrialisation which viewed people as 'the masses' to be set in motion or sacrificed by an omniscient Party for the long-term benefit of future generations; and its mirror image, bourgeois political economy – the soulless application of market forces to generate economic growth regardless of human cost.

This work, more than any other single text, inspired the great explosion of historical endeavour represented in such institutions as History Workshop, feminist historiography, and the historiography of previously marginalised groups – even when Thompson's successors took strong issue with his particular interpretations or emphases. Even as late as 1981, Bill Schwartz expressed apprehension that discussion of the CP Historians' Group might appear excessively provincial – such a suggestion would be unthinkable now.

❑ Contents of Issue 8

The articles and reviews in this issue of *Socialist History* are indicative of the wide range of historical forces with which the work of the British Marxist historians have intersected. We begin with John Callaghan's examination of the road to the climactic moment of 1956 and, in the other main articles, go on to examine aspects of the work of the historians themselves, in each case trying to establish a fresh and hitherto unexamined perspective. Harvey Kaye has become the most eminent commentator on the tradition and its members – he contributes a fresh assessment of Thompson's importance together with some personal insights. What has not, until now, been much studied in relation to Thompson's work is the period he spent as an extra-mural tutor in Yorkshire, the aspect which is taken up by Andy Croft. Raymond Williams is placed in relation to the tradition by Stephen Woodhams. The publication of Eric Hobsbawm's *Age of Extremes* in 1994 provoked a great deal of discussion and a number of interviews with the author. In one of these, given to the BBC and reprinted in this number, he discusses not only the book itself but what it has meant to be a Marxist historian. The large number of reviews which appear in this issue relate either directly to the theme of the title, the international movement in which they were formed, or else range across the various fields of historical research that have developed from the historiographical turmoil of 40 years ago.

Willie Thompson

NOTES

1. The word 'history' is derived from the French *histoire*. It does not mean 'his story' and has no gender connotations.
2. See for example Raphael Samuel, 'British Marxist Historians', *New Left Review*, 120.
3. What might be termed the quasi-Marxist *Annales* school of historiography was also a fresh creation of the interwar years.
4. Eric Hobsbawm, 'The Historians' Group of the Communist Party' in M. Cornforth, ed., *Rebels and their Causes* (Lawrence and Wishart, 1978); Bill Schwartz, '"The People" in history: the Communist Party Historians' Group, 1946–56', in R. Johnson et al, eds, *Making Histories* (Hutchinson, 1982); Harvey Kaye, *The British Marxist Historians* (Polity Press, 1984).
5. See Andy Croft, 'Authors Take Sides: Writers and the Communist Party 1920–56', in Geoff Andrews et al, eds, *Opening the Books: Essays on the Social and Cultural History of the British Communist Party* (Pluto Press, 1995).
6. Interestingly, the history of the British labour movement by A.L. Morton and George Tate, published by Lawrence and Wishart in the 1950s, ends at 1920.

THE ROAD TO 1956

John Callaghan

KHRUSHCHEV'S 'SECRET SPEECH' TO the Twentieth Congress of the Communist Party of the Soviet Union (CPSU) in February 1956 opened a window for communists by allowing them to see at least something of the true nature of the Stalin regime; Soviet repression of the uprising in Hungary later in the year demonstrated the limitations of that vision by showing that 'Stalinism' had outlived Stalin and could not be explained by the 'cult of personality'. The obvious questions to ask are: why did it take a General Secretary of the CPSU to open communist eyes and why did so many communists continue to keep them shut? The answer offered here – elaborated in relation to the CPGB – is rooted in a historical analysis of the communist movement and communist identity.

❑ A 'war party'

The Communist Party was conceived as a war party. The First World War paved the way for its creation both by disillusioning a proportion of the militant left with Social Democratic principles of party organisation and providing in the Bolshevik Revolution proof of the efficacy of insurrection. Lenin emerged as a figure with international authority because the apparent success of his own party contrasted so sharply with the lamentable record of social democracy. The Bolsheviks had opposed the imperialist war and taken state power in the name of international socialism; the social democrats, on the other hand, had supported the futile slaughter waged by rival capitalist states. Lenin's adamantine anti-imperialism had been seen to work while other varieties of socialism and Marxism, it was argued, had either capitulated or equivocated. Much Bolshevik propaganda at the time of the formation of the Communist International (Comintern) in 1919, moreover, was designed to show that those in the 'middle' – socialists who opposed the war but rejected Leninism – were no better than the 'social imperialists'. When the Comintern adopted its 21 conditions of membership in 1920, they were designed in large measure to exclude just such people.

The militants who founded the communist parties did so in the immediate aftermath of a war which was widely perceived to have been more than an unparalleled disaster; it was a turning point in history.[1] It marked the end of liberal confidence in gradual, orderly progress and was evidence for many intellectuals drawn from this tradition of the advent of powerful – seemingly uncontrollable – irrational forces. Lenin's claim that the war was evidence of an unfolding imperialist epoch characterised by 'wars, civil wars, and revolutions' should be situated in this context. Such doom-laden convictions fed the 'messianic sectarianism' which impelled the militant left towards Bolshevism, as the Hungarian communist, Gyorgy Lukacs, remembered from the time of his own 'conversion' to the revolution. For such intransigent spirits Lenin's Marxism was the one doctrine which showed a way out of the mess.[2] The October Revolution and the universally applicable precepts which had made it possible were now seized upon in a spirit of religious zeal by men and women of the dissident minority. After years of apparently futile opposition to the war, from marginal groups or powerless factions of the labour movement, the militants rallied to a revolution and a doctrine which had redeemed socialism, vindicated their own beliefs and promised to place them centre-stage in the unfolding drama. The problem now was to become Bolshevik oneself and to learn the appropriate lessons.

Of course there were socialists who were repelled by Bolshevik methods. After coming into contact with the Bolsheviks for the first time at the end of 1919 at an international students' conference in Geneva, Ellen Wilkinson said 'this is the most ghastly, callous, inhuman machine I have ever witnessed'. But Rajani Palme Dutt to whom she expressed this opinion was attracted to the Bolsheviks precisely because they advocated methods which 'mean business' – methods which showed they were as organised and disciplined as the enemy.[3] The contrast with the old type of Marxist group was vivid enough; these now seemed inept and amateurish by comparison with Lenin's vanguard party. Thus when Lenin introduced the celebrated '21 conditions of membership' to ensure that the recently formed Third International was composed of communist parties modelled on the Bolsheviks, militants like Dutt and Harry Pollitt were ready to give themselves totally to the job of imitation. Already veterans of the 'Hands Off Russia' campaign it goes without saying that they enthusiastically volunteered that spirit of 'unconditional defence of the Soviet Republic' now formally demanded of them.

It was the combination of 'the strictest internal discipline' and an external policy of 'revolutionary opportunism' which had persuaded Dutt that the Bolsheviks meant business.[4] The Communist International (Comintern) was fashioned as a single world party. It presupposed not only the desirability of a single directing centre for the world workers' movement but also that the capitalist world economy had created sufficiently homogeneous conditions to make such central direction feasible and effective. The national 'sections' or parties were thus subordinate to an Executive Committee whose rulings were binding. Within the national sections themselves a rigorous centralisation and iron discipline was also the aspiration from the beginning – if not, at first, the reality. Nothing less than military cohesion would meet the challenge of the predicted civil wars in which the communists would be pitched against the forces of the state – an increasingly authoritarian state at that, according to Lenin's *Imperialism*, in many ways the foundation document of the new International.[5]

❏ No scruples

The hard business of wresting power away from the hated representatives of capital left no room for scruple; legality or illegality, one manoeuvre or another – it was just a question of tactics. This is what Dutt meant by 'revolutionary opportunism' but it would be missing a great deal if we were to pass this by without mentioning the scientific precision which communists claimed for changes in the tactical line determined by the Comintern.[6] Leninism, in the received view, was nothing unless it was a science of tactics. Certainty prevailed then on at least two counts of accepted doctrine; history had created the material foundations of capitalist decay while the party – the 'Modern Prince' in Gramsci's telling phrase – possessed the craft to establish its hegemony and canalise the workers' struggle. Truth was with the communists and Marxism – and at Bolshevik insistence the truth was understood as a total world-view covering nature and society. When we remember, in addition, that the theatre of bourgeois morality was held to rest on foundations of bullshit then we can understand how easy it was to deduce from all of this that there was no utility in an independent morality outside the class struggle, even if one entertained the thought that such a morality might exist. And so, as Trotsky later observed, for as long as class struggle existed, lying and violence were inevitable and permissible weapons in the party's armoury.[7] Few in the ranks would have realised that in the amoral conditions of the war against capitalist society the communist leaders would sometimes see fit to lie to their own side.

Stories of the ruthless cruelty of the new Bolshevik regime littered the press in the first years of Lenin's power. Communists learned to live with such talk even when it came from figures on the left such as the anarchist Emma Goldman, who toured Britain in 1924.[8] The tough-minded knew that a revolution could not be made without violence. Harry Pollitt, for example, was prominent among those at the Labour Party conference in 1922 who defended the Bolshevik death sentences hanging over the 47 socialist revolutionaries.[9] The new regime had to defend itself from enemies within and without. In the global offensive against capitalism furthermore, it was understood that the Soviet Republic represented the only offensive position. It had to be defended at all costs. Relief would come when the expected breakthrough in Western Europe materialised. That in turn depended on the successful assimilation of Bolshevism or the construction of the Party – it was much the same thing. Those who really wanted democracy to flourish in Russia, it was argued, should do nothing to strengthen its international isolation and everything to break the capitalist grip in their own lands. With the passing years, in fact, the defence of the Soviet Republic acquired additional significance precisely as the prospects for advance in Germany – long considered the weakest front in the capitalist West – actually receded after 1921. But as the Bolsheviks held on to state power, so the repression of their opponents intensified. The conflation of state, party and class to which communists were inclined from the outset hardened into doctrine as the last formal opposition to the Party was swept away in practice at the end of the civil war.

Communists appreciated that the painful exigencies of Bolshevik isolation in the world states system constrained the Soviet Republic to manoeuvre for its very survival. Realism dictated that the retention of state power was what mattered, not the unfortunate but necessary jettisoning of this or that principle or policy. To the accusation that the communist parties were simply instruments of Soviet foreign policy Otto Kuusinen replied in 1924 that any such assistance would only be a matter for celebration.[10] He was not contradicted in the communist press.

❑ Precarious survival

In Britain the communists were busy establishing a precarious toe-hold from 1920, conscious that even this depended on the material assistance and ideological authority of the Soviet state and the Comintern. Soviet democracy was on the brink of extinction when this project began. Just four years later the British Party was no nearer realising its early ambitions when the factional struggle in Russia, following Lenin's death, saw the majority of Bolshevik leaders line up against Trotsky's faction. No one could guess how far Trotsky had yet to fall but it must have been immediately apparent that the slender prospects for communism in Britain would not be improved by the appearance of sympathetic divisions in the British Party. The leadership was in any case at one with the Comintern in the expectation of an immediate improvement in the CPGB's prospects during the two years leading up to the General Strike of 1926. There was every reason to concentrate on the task in hand. Even after the TUC's abject defeat, the Comintern continued to predict a sharpening of the class struggle in Britain and an immediate upsurge in support for communism. Though this argument met with resistance it reinforced the position of sectarians like Dutt and those such as Pollitt and Shapurji Saklatvala who realised that purges against the communists left only a contracting space for the old policy of work within the mass organisations of labour. In the event, of course, the entire International was set on a disastrous turn of ultra-leftism in 1928. It had to be imposed on the CPGB and there is ample evidence of continued resistance and scepticism within the leadership until the policy was belatedly reversed in 1935.[11]

❑ Loyalties

What kept the communists loyal to the Comintern in these circumstances? For Dutt and Pollitt the explanation is simply that they supported most aspects of the Comintern's position. In addition, Pollitt became General Secretary of the Party in 1929 undoubtedly with Soviet-Comintern assistance. But it is equally important to remember that Pollitt's elevation was supported inside the CPGB as a step in the completion of the 'Bolshevisation' of the Party that had begun in 1922. It is a reminder that for most people in the British Party – Dutt included – the belief persisted that progress depended on the 'correct' organisation and tactics. The dissidents who rejected the Comintern's New Line were no different on this matter; they simply disagreed with current perspectives. But on this, as on subsequent occasions when the line changed more or less abruptly, even those with grave doubts and misgivings saw the merit of disciplined acquiescence. It was not a matter of blindly following the Bolshevik lead, though no doubt there was an element of 'the Bolsheviks know best' in their reasoning; but it must be remembered that the leaders had joined a centralised International in 1920 because August 1914 had shown that disaster followed when strict observance of international resolutions was absent. They were also revolutionaries without affection for the Labour Party and in Britain there was nowhere else to go. Above all they believed in Lenin's vision of the times in which they lived. It was indeed a period of successive crises which could plausibly detonate systemic breakdown and provide objective grounds for revolutionary optimism. In short, even if one questioned shifts in Comintern tactics there were compelling ideological grounds for loyalty to the movement.

From the late 1920s until 1945 the claims of communist discipline drew heavily on the international fascist threat. In the same period communist confidence drew massively on the success of Soviet planning and the apparent breakdown of the capitalist world economy. The argument that Stalin's transformation of the Soviet economy had laid the foundations for all manner of cultural advances was heard well beyond the confines of the communist parties. The left's confidence in the primacy of the economic base as a cause of historical progress explains why it was possible to judge in favour of the Soviet Union, even if the reports of rigged trials, terror and cruelty were believed. It could be reasoned that unsavoury aspects of the political system were the legacy of Russia's former backwardness, the inevitable results of international isolation, the necessary means required to force-march the economy and that, in time, economic advance would undermine the dictatorship by producing an educated, urbanised working class on an enormous scale to replace the passive, illiterate peasantry of old. What communists calculated in private, some of Stalin's critics openly announced; that Stalinism would be undermined by the economic advances brutally inaugurated by Stalin.

We now know that members of the Party's Central Committee expressed their own doubts about the authenticity of the Moscow Trials and that at various times in the 1930s there was 'talk of the collapse of the International, talk of the Soviet Union following its interests and the like, talk of our being an independent Party, all kinds of things like that'.[12] It underlines the point that the doubters remained communists because they made a judgement that the progressive forces would prevail. The great strides made by Soviet planning, the victories of the Red Army, the postwar lurch to the left in Europe, the spread of Soviet power, the advance of communism in Asia – surely this was evidence that the old mole of history was doing its work?

❑ Lost illusions

Even in Britain the prospects for socialism had never looked brighter than they appeared in the first year after the Second World War. By that time the CPGB had experienced ten years of Popular Frontism and was bigger, and in some ways more pluralistic, than at any time in its history. The signs were already visible that the old monolithic conception of the communist movement was dying. Stalin had dissolved the Comintern in 1943, the talk was now of various 'national roads' to socialism and communists belonged to coalition governments in a number of European states. But from 1947 the Cold War nipped this process of disintegration in the bud and communists closed ranks. If the perceived political choices were reduced to communism and its enemies, now was not the time to criticise one's own side. The bipolarity of world politics in these Cold War conditions gave a new relevance and life to the war-party of old. It created circumstances in which a new wave of Stalinist terror was able to reduce the ranks in Eastern Europe while maintaining the loyalties, if not always the credulity, of those in the movement who looked on.

The latest generation of purges and show trials which swept across Eastern Europe in the period 1948–53, not to mention the excommunication and abrupt rehabilitation of Tito's Yugoslavia, certainly troubled consciences. They gave added empirical weight to the reports of systematic persecution and cruelty in Stalin's Russia which former communists such as Victor Serge, Arthur Koestler, Walter Krivitsky and Margareta Buber-Neuman added in the 1940s to the burgeoning literature in the English language concerned with Soviet totalitarianism. Not all of this was easily dismissed as Cold War propaganda. But few British communists allowed their unease to take them publicly out of the Party or bring them into open conflict with it; and those who did – such as Douglas Hyde and C.H. Darke – provoked a mixture of anger and pity among their former comrades as their stories were taken up by the enemy and used to discredit the cause. Only when Khrushchev denounced 'Stalin's crimes' from within the citadel itself was it possible for some of the foot soldiers of communism to bring their doubts and misgivings into focus. The depth of the betrayal cost the Party almost one-third of its membership by the end of 1957.

The old leaders who had slipped, by degrees, into the habits of mind and organisation which made them complicit in the maintenance of Stalinism were incapable of a constructive response to Khrushchev's revelations. Dutt initially hoped that the whole episode would blow over, possibly after Khrushchev lost his power struggle within the CPSU. If he ever did comprehend the scale of the Stalinist disaster, he never admitted it — he was in any case frankly amoral, trusting that the caravan of history would roll on irrespective of 'Stalin's crimes', repeating Engels to the effect that a revolution was necessarily authoritarian.[13] Others, like Willie Gallacher and Harry Pollitt, suffered from shock as well as incomprehension.[14] Khrushchev himself had provided the formula, however, for readjustment; the 'crimes' had done nothing to damage the fundamentally progressive character of the society Stalin had done so much to fashion. Twenty years later John Gollan, Pollitt's successor as General Secretary, looked in retrospect at the Twentieth Congress and repeated the argument; 'the basic socialist foundations of the Soviet Union', he asserted, 'were unshaken despite the crimes in the period of Stalin's leadership'.[15] Twenty years after the monolith had suffered its most decisive crack, the Party was admittedly unable to cohere around this formula. It would take Gorbachev to finally bury it.

John Callaghan teaches at Wolverhampton University. His most recent book is Rajani Palme Dutt: A Study in British Stalinism.

NOTES

1. See for example, S. Hynes, *A War Imagined: The First World War and English Culture* (Pimlico, 1990).
2. G. Lukacs, *Record of a Life*, ed. Istvan Estori, trans. R. Livingstone (1983), p. 76.
3. R. Palme Dutt, 'Rough Draft of Some Experiences of the Communist International and the Period of Stalin's Leading Role', Confidential MS, Easter

1970, p. 2, CPGB archive; See also Anon., 'Reminiscences of Palme Dutt', *Our History Journal*, no. 11 January 1987, p. 5.

4. R. Palme Dutt, 'Communism', *Encyclopaedia Britannica*, 12th edition 1925.

5. See F. Claudin, *The Communist Movement* (Peregrine, 1975) and N. Harding, *Lenin's Political Thought* Volume Two, *Theory and Practice in the Socialist Revolution* (Macmillan, 1981).

6. For evidence of this assertion see R. Palme Dutt, *Lenin* (Hamish Hamilton, 1933), p. 10 and the same author's *Leninism* (Marx Memorial Library, 1941), pp. 3–4.

7. L. Trotsky, *Their Morals and Ours* (Pathfinder, 1969), p. 28.

8. See M. Durham, 'British Revolutionaries and the Suppression of the Left in Lenin's Russia 1918–1924', *Journal of Contemporary History*, vol. 20, 1985.

9. *Labour Party Annual Conference Report*, 1922.

10. O. Kuusinen, 'Under the Leadership of Russia', *Communist International*, Jubilee number 1, 1924, p. 134.

11. J. Callaghan, *Rajani Palme Dutt* (Lawrence and Wishart, 1993), chapter 4.

12. F. King and G. Matthews, *About Turn: The Communist Party and the Outbreak of the Second World War* (Lawrence and Wishart, 1990), p. 86.

13. J. Callaghan, *Rajani Palme Dutt*, chapter 8.

14. See K. Morgan, *Harry Pollitt* (Manchester University Press, 1993).

15. J. Gollan, 'Socialist Democracy – Some Problems: The Twentieth Congress in Retrospect', *Marxism Today*, January 1976, p. 5.

WALTHAMSTOW, LITTLE GIDDING AND MIDDLESBROUGH: EDWARD THOMPSON, ADULT EDUCATION AND LITERATURE

Andy Croft

Most of living is driving through fog to badly attended classes to give ill-prepared lectures.
   Edward Thompson to Randall Swingler, 22 January 1959.

AS WE APPROACH THE fortieth anniversary of the events of 1956, there are unlikely to be many attempts to vindicate the Soviet decision to invade Hungary (though there will, no doubt, be those who wish to find new reasons to justify the occupation of Suez). The collapse of the Soviet Union and of the Warsaw Pact has hardly strengthened the position of those who believed that Socialism could be built with someone else's tanks. The drama inside the British Communist Party in 1956 – part Greek Tragedy, part comic-opera – is now too familiar to require rehearsing again, and has anyway lost any lingering political resonance since the dissolution of the Party. It all seems a very long time ago, the vivid memoirs of some of the surviving participants reaching us like messages from a long-exploded star. Meanwhile a number of welcome new studies of the period have begun to look beyond 1956, reconsidering the way those events shaped the beginnings of the New Left, representing either the end of the communist tradition, the liberation of that tradition from Stalinism, or the strangling at birth of a post-Stalinist left by the good intentions of ex-communists with old habits.[1]

Whatever the merits of these interpretations, each seems to imply, to a greater or lesser extent, that '1956' was a crisis waiting to erupt in the British Party. The Twentieth Congress, the invasion of Hungary and the disastrous handling of the crisis by the Party leadership: these were simply the sparks which lit the blue touch-paper of discontent among Party members. Yet it is clear that many of those who left the Party in 1956 or 1957 neither wanted nor expected to leave; on the contrary, many felt, initially at least, that events had given them renewed reason to be communists and new hope for the British Party, liberated from the demonstrably corrupt consequences of Stalinism. By the mid-1950s, British communists were used to failure, isolation and decline; few can have imagined they were likely to be on the 'winning side' in the Cold War (whatever that might have meant). Bad news from Moscow was by then hardly new. Most Party intellectuals were anyway wearily habituated to conflicts with King Street, conflicts which increasingly defined the relationship of a number of intellectuals to the Party. By forcing the British Party into a defensive, embattled and internalised political culture, the Cold War had arguably served to *stabilise* the British Party (at the same time as cutting it off from any real hope of advance). The crisis of '1956', in other words, was arguably more unexpected than historians of the New Left sometimes assume.

What follows provides an account of part of the working life in the late 1940s and 1950s of one of the key figures of 1956, which suggests, perhaps, some of the reasons why '1956' did not happen earlier, why one independent-minded intellectual living and working a long way from King Street remained in the Party through the worst years of the 'Battle of Ideas'. It is a sideways glance at the Communist Party's cultural life during the Cold War, and a reminder of the extent to which contemporary literary culture seemed to be in such crisis as to justify some of the worst excesses of Zhdanovism. It indicates, perhaps, some of the sources of Thompson's 'cultural populism' and the ideas which he took into the New Left (and beyond) as well as the habit of polemic which distinguished his later writings. These were the years in which Thompson 'made himself', as a teacher, as a historian and as a 'reasoning' Marxist; when he found himself engaged in a 'a war on two fronts' and chose the intellectual terrain (and the moral high ground) on which he was to fight some of his most famous battles.

It is also a study of adult education in the Cold War, one of the few fronts in the 'Battle of Ideas' where communists were not completely defeated (and later one of the key sources of intellectual renewal in the New Left). It may be a reminder that, even at the height of the Cold War, adult education was a rather more dynamic and open intellectual space than it is now. Thompson's warnings about the corruption of adult education by the universities makes uncomfortable reading in the light of HEFC(E) circular 3/94 and the Gadarene rush towards Accreditation, Modularisation and Mainstreaming.

❏ 'The tutor fell down badly'

Not surprisingly, perhaps, it is sometimes forgotten that Edward Thompson began his academic career teaching literature. And yet for much of his time at Leeds (1948–1965), Thompson clearly saw literature as his primary subject, himself as a poet and literary criticism as the most effective means of intervening in contemporary British cultural and political life.

After demobilisation Thompson spent a year studying English literature at Cambridge, before applying in 1948 for the post of staff tutor in the newly-formed Extra-Mural Department at Leeds, where he offered to teach history, political science, international relations and literature, which he said had long been his chief interest, both in attempts as a practising writer and as a field of study. Over the next 16 years, Edward Thompson taught courses in literature for the Department in Ossett, Shepley, Bingley, Cleckheaton, Batley, Leeds, Halifax, Middlesbrough, Harrogate and Morley (as well as single lectures, day-schools, weekend schools and summer schools). For the first three years, *all* Thompson's classes were in literature; there was no time when he was not teaching at least one literature class. In each of the years he was writing *The Making of the English Working Class* (between 1959 and 1962) he taught literature classes in Harrogate, Halifax and Morley, and only one class in history.[2]

On the whole, Thompson's literature courses seem, on paper at least, to have been conventional enough for their time. Always working with a WEA branch, and usually beginning with a preparatory year, he worked with the same students for a period of three of four years, negotiating the next year's syllabus with the class according to their interests and his sense of their developing critical abilities, and of their collective capacity for reading. Wide-ranging, ambitious and suggestive, his classes typically alternated between close textual study and synoptic sweeps around those nineteenth-century and early twentieth-century texts that were already, perhaps, becoming canonical in adult education – *Wuthering Heights, Hard Times, Mary Barton, Jude the Obscure*, Owen and Lawrence. Apart from some classes in Elizabethan literature, his courses were devoted on the whole, to the study of poetry and fiction, rarely to drama (the only playwrights he appears to have taught were O'Casey, Synge, Galsworthy, Auden and later Wesker, although most classes studied a Shakespeare play, usually as an introduction to literary study).

One of his first classes for the Department was in Bingley in 1949–50 where, the syllabus announced,

> The central theme will be an examination of various aspects of the writer's technique and of the use of Literary criticism. We will first discuss the problems raised in selected passages of prose and individual poems. We will then follow these problems in a discussion of two or three novels. And finally we will study a few important poems and passages of prose and criticism written during the period in which the Industrial society of today was coming into being.

It is not clear from the syllabus what the 'problems' were which the class pursued from Palgrave's *Golden Treasury* to Dickens, though Thompson's frequent aim seems to have been to draw the attention of the class to issues of creativity, subjectivity and responsibility. After considering 'the materials of literature':

> Various meanings of words – advertisements, headlines, speeches. Scientific precision and poetic precision. Rhythm, imagery, and music. Judgements of value – subjective and technical use and limitations of criticism. The facts which are relevant to a study of literature and the facts with which we are not concerned.

The course moved through 'a brief discussion of the social function of literature' (looking at early ballads, poetry by Marvell, Owen and Yeats) to 'a discussion of the amount of selection and control the writer imposes on his material in the novel form' (*Wuthering Heights* and *Hard Times*) concluding with a look at poetry by Blake, Wordsworth, Byron and Shelley, criticism by Wordsworth, Shelley, Hazlitt and Leigh Hunt, a 'general examination of the "romantic movement" in outline' and 'a more detailed study of poems and letters by John Keats'.

Most of Thompson's courses relied on this kind of grand and eclectic approach, impressively – and impossibly – ambitious in trying to balance his own enthusiasms and those of his students with his perception of the needs of the class. The third year of his Middlesbrough class in 1955–56, for example, aimed to cover 'Shakespeare and *King Lear*' (looking at Marlowe and Jonson on the way) *and* 'The European Novel' (Cervantes, Fielding, Flaubert, Tolstoy, Dostoievsky) *and* 'Recent English Literature' – and all in 24 weeks. Thompson's courses were not typically constructed around a close study of a historical period, though his third year 'Modern Literature and Practical Criticism' courses in Cleckheaton and Batley in 1950–51 did try to sprint from *Jude the Obscure* and *Heart of Darkness* through the 1920s and 1930s towards 'the cultural situation today'.

The only real exception to this pattern were the occasional courses he taught in Elizabethan literature (second year courses in Cleckheaton and Batley in 1949–50 and Bingley in 1951–52 and a third year course in Leeds in 1953–54). And these were, if anything, more ambitious still. The first three evenings of 'Aspects of Elizabethan Literature' in Bingley for example, required students to read *Utopia, Everyman* and poetry by Spenser, Wyatt and Sidney (with *Don Quixote*, Drake's *The World Encompassed* and *The Prince* as further reading); by the fourth week they were discussing *The Chester Pageant of the Deluge* and *Tamburlaine*; *Dr Faustus* and Sidney's *Apology for Poetry* by week seven; after a lecture on the Elizabethan theatre in week eight the course settled down to a closer study of Marlowe (including *Hero and Leander, Edward II* and – as a contrast – *Richard II*), Bacon, Nashe and Donne, before accelerating off again through *The Alchemist, King Lear, Timon of Athens* and *Volpone*.

Thompson soon realised he was expecting too much reading of his students. Reporting on the Cleckheaton Elizabethan literature class he admitted that 'the unfamiliar work made progress appear slow at first'. Though he regretted that few students had read the 'further reading' suggested in the syllabus, he blamed himself for the slow progress of the class. Too many lectures, he felt, were arranged for the imparting of information, and students were reluctant to make judgements on questions on which they felt they were insufficiently informed, or informed only at second-hand by the tutor: they were provided with too few opportunities to grapple with material and work out the essentials for themselves, in writing and discussion.

'I would blush to mention the number of texts "touched upon"', he wrote of his Shipley course in 1950–51, 'ranging from Dekker's *Shoemaker's Holiday* to Carlyle's *Past and Present*, from Marvell's *Horation Ode* to Yeats' *Easter 1916*. Looking back on a fourth year class on 'European Literature' in Batley in 1951–52 – which concentrated on close readings of *Don Quixote, Gulliver's Travels, Pilgrim's Progress, Tom Jones, Madame Bovary, The Idiot* and *The Brothers Karamazov* (with background texts by Chaucer, Rabelais, Nashe, Bunyan, Defoe, Richardson, Sterne, Smollett and Voltaire) – he acknowledged that the course had been too ambitious, particularly since 'this considerable slab of meat was sandwiched in between *Antony and Cleopatra* at the beginning, and a couple of evenings of William Morris at the end':

> Since the tutor fell down badly on the programme he had set himself, there is no wonder that most of the class lagged very far behind ... there were moments in the year when both tutor and students began to find this cross-country race rather heavy going ...

This is typical of his early Class Reports, where he catalogued, with touching frankness, the frustrations and disappointments of teaching adults as well as a sense of his own shortcomings. 'It has been hard work keeping this class alert and interested', he wrote of his first year at Shepley, 'while at the same time persuading the students to carry on work of a satisfactory standard':

> Several of them remain responsive only to a very narrow range of literature: they are confused by any unorthodox or frank approach to personal or sexual morality: one persists in praising Warwick Deeping and in referring to Shakespeare as 'high-brow stuff': the others are certainly happier with Mrs Gaskell or Galsworthy than with D. H. Lawrence or poetry of any description. The same students are puzzled and offended when presented with exercises and are happiest if the evening is made up of an hour's talkative lecture providing starting-points for a further hour of diffuse discussion on any subject under the sun – even (on occasions) literature.

He soon learned the difficulty of judging his response to those students who showed a desire for something more than this. In Bingley in 1949–50 he reported that he had responded too quickly to the best students, unsuccessfully urging them to attempt a close analysis of the development of Keats' poetry over a six-week period.

Thompson was clearly happiest teaching poetry, and frequently reported problems in teaching fiction ('without any doubt the form of literature which lends itself least readily to class discussion'). At Shepley in 1948–49 he blamed himself for the failure of the class to respond to *Sons and Lovers*; 'the tutor's inexperience in working out a satisfactory technique for studying the novel may have contributed to this'. As a result, 'several students persisted until the end in isolating moral or political problems and discussing them irrespective of their context in the work under discussion'. Again, in Middlesbrough in 1954–55, he felt the responsibility for a disappointing year lay in his teaching of the novels on the syllabus (though to be fair to Thompson they had been reading *Heart of Midlothian*):

My own teaching has tended to be a bit dim this year, especially when dealing with the novels on the syllabus: on two occasions I did not find the time to thoroughly re-read the novels under discussion immediately prior to the class meetings (a necessity for fresh teaching) and reliance on recollections and two or three-year-old notes was no substitute.

Possibly to address this sense of weakness, he invited Arnold Kettle, then in the University's English Department (and the Communist Party) to talk to his classes in Batley and Cleckheaton in 1950–51 on the modern novel; in 1949-50, Kenneth Muir visited Thompson's class in Cleckheaton to talk about editing Shakespeare; in 1961–62 John Braine sat in on a discussion about *Room at the Top* among Thompson's students in Morley.

But teaching drama was not without its problems, either. At the end of his first year in Ossett, Thompson reported that he had made 'the serious mistake of giving in to the vocal demand for play-reading from his women students':

> Far too much time was given to reading the plays in class, thus discouraging the student's private study of texts. Few students attempted background reading, and the tutor's own background lectures seem, in retrospect, to have been sketchy and to have failed in enthusiasm.

This identification of a leisurely, provincial philistinism with women students is one of the most striking features of his early Class Reports (his solution to the problems of the Ossett class was to recruit more men). He consciously planned the second year of his course in Bingley in 1950–51 – *The City of Dreadful Night, The Way of All Flesh, Major Barbara, Jude the Obscure, Father and Son, The Private Papers of Henry Ryecroft, Revolution in Tanner's Lane, News from Nowhere,* Morris' *Essays on Art and Socialism, Erewhon, The Story of my Heart* and poems by Owen, Hopkins, Bridges and Lawrence – in the hope that it 'might attract trade unionists to the class and redress the house-wife and professional bias' of the first year (it did not). In his first year at Shepley he found the class divided between:

> ... a group of four or five men predominantly interested in political and social problems, and all active in the trade union and labour movement; and a slightly larger group of women, several of whom desired entertaining performances from the tutor (covering with

equal authority the details of a writer's private life and questions of literary value) culminating in literary gossip in the discussion period.

To be fair, Thompson was equally dismayed by the attitude of the men in the class who criticised Emily Brontë for not being Dickens and who 'persisted in regarding poetry as a luxury the labour movement could do without'. And both caricatures were presumably an expression of his own frustrated expectations – at least in his first years in the Department – of teaching an idealised Northern industrial working class. The absence of trade unionists in particular he repeatedly lamented in his Class Reports. He was, for example, clearly disappointed by the social composition of his first class in proletarian Middlesbrough:

> The class might almost equally well have been held in Walthamstow, Little Gidding, or Middlesbrough, for all the special common experience, interests, or community sense to be found in the group. Two steelworkers (it is true) were on the provisional register: but, despite the friendly atmosphere of the class, they did not appear to be at home, and did not go beyond the sixth meeting ... the tutor, who drove over eighty miles to the illuminated sky and glaring furnaces of the steel centres, found this disappointing ...

❑ **Intolerable opinions**

If Thompson spent a good deal of time in these years journeying in hope to Teesside, he also travelled a great deal back and forth between Little Gidding and Walthamstow, between T.S. Eliot and William Morris. They represented for him opposing ideas of poetry, as well as antagonistic visions of Tradition and England. But while adult students often expected him to include Eliot (then at the height of his influence and authority) in the syllabus, there was a reluctance to study Morris, generally assumed to be, as Thompson later put it, an unreadable 'old fuddy-duddy'.[3] During all the years he was writing the Morris book, he included Morris on the syllabus of only two courses. Eliot however, frequently appeared in his reading lists, usually as an example of 'Tradition and Reaction in Modern Literature' as in his Bingley class of 1952–53. In 1950–51 Eliot was included on the syllabus of both his Cleckheaton and Batley classes; at Batley, where the class contained more professional and middle-class students than usual, he was clearly disappointed that they liked Eliot rather more than Lawrence; at Cleckheaton however, Thompson was pleased to report that 'the class began to yawn as evenings went by on *The Waste Land*, and students began to suggest that we were spending too much time on a lifeless and pretentious document of literary history'. When Roy Shaw and Richard Hoggart ran a weekend school in 1951 on 'T.S. Eliot: Poet of Our Time', Thompson criticised their choice of title – 'while Mr Eliot may be a great poet (and in my opinion he is not) he is no longer a contemporary poet', urging the Department to vary its 'well established Forster–Woolf–Joyce–Eliot–Yeats kind of menu'.

The critique of Eliot and the whole 'negative reaction' of Modernism derived in part from his earlier involvement in the Communist Party Writers' Group, where he had moved among an older generation of communist poets like Randall Swingler, Jack Lindsay and Edgell Rickword.[4] It was one of the forcefully expressed arguments of the Communist Party's cultural journal *Our Time*, edited then by Rickword, later by Swingler, to which Thompson began contributing poetry and poetry criticism.[5] In the political climate of the first years of peace, intellectual debate, particularly on cultural questions, flourished inside the Party. At a meeting of the Writers' Group in 1945, for example, Thompson (and George Thomson) defended an unorthodox attempt by Jack Lindsay to revise reductive applications of the Base-Superstructure model of Marxist theories of culture.[6] But the Cold War was closing in, and by 1947 David Holbrook, Arnold Rattenbury (whom Thompson knew from school) and Thompson himself were pressing for *Our Time* to take a more polemical, anti-American line. Emile Burns, Chair of the Party's Cultural Committee took the opportunity to remove Rickword as editor, and the magazine made a sharp 'left' turn under an editorial commission of Young Turks.[7]

By then, however, Thompson had moved to the West Riding. Although he was active in the Communist Party – in his Party branch and on the Yorkshire District Committee, chair of the Halifax Peace Committee, Secretary of Yorkshire Federation of Peace Organisations and editor of *Yorkshire Voice of Peace* – his sense of himself as an active communist during these years seems to have been principally defined by literature, by teaching and writing, and by his attempts to write poetry. He occasionally read his poems at poetry readings at Marx House, and in 1950 he entered a long poem to the Festival of Britain poetry competition, partly about the Atom Bomb, partly about the failure of contemporary poetry to respond adequately to the implications of nuclear weapons.[8]

Thompson started writing this poem – which of course was not among the winners – while staying with the Swinglers in Essex. In these years Randall Swingler's friendship was clearly important to him, a communist poet with whom (like Tom McGrath) he could discuss contemporary poetry and the poetry he was trying to write. For Thompson was increasingly dissatisfied with his own verse, which he considered too shrill and superficially political, swinging between wild and angry invective and sentimentality, and was struggling to write a new kind of lyrical poetry. He still hoped that the intellectual sclerosis of the Cold War might prove temporary, and that the Party could intervene successfully in British cultural life. In 1951 he contributed a poem to *Arena*, edited by Swingler and Lindsay, about the fall of Seoul, looking back to Blake.[9]

When in 1951 Swingler and Lindsay planned a new literary journal to replace *Arena*, he urged them to fight for the proposal over the heads of the Cultural Committee at the Political Committee, stressing the need for the Party to launch a new literary journal which could give a lead to contemporary poets in the way the Party had done during the late 1930s. That year Swingler gave Thompson the opportunity of reviewing poetry for the *Daily Worker*. He was also occasionally invited to write (over his own name) Walter Holmes' famous 'Worker's Notebook' column in the paper:

> The lion is not yet roused. But the town of Ben Rushton and Ralph Fox has still some history to make. This time the signs will not prove false. We are about to see one of the those astonishing awakenings of British history. When it comes it will surprise even ourselves. Halifax will soon be going up on the 'moor' again. There the Chartists and the Radicals and early Socialists held their monster meetings. When this happens it will mean that the plans of the warmakers are finished for once and for all.[10]

Thompson also wrote a pamphlet on the history of newspapers for the *Daily Worker*:

> The national dailies, in their search for the sensational and the corrupt, fasten upon the wildest rumour or most trivial incident, seize every pretext to inflame misunderstanding between ourselves and the Russian people. Commercial journalism (like British film stars) is

beginning to affect an American accent, and British readers are served up with columns eulogising the 'American Way of Life' ... Only the *Daily Worker* ...[11]

❏ William Morris

In 1951 he contributed a long essay on 'The Murder of William Morris' to *Arena*, and gave a splendidly anti-American paper on 'William Morris and the Moral Issues Today' at the Party's Cultural Committee conference on 'The American Threat to British Liberty' invoking Literature, Communism and teaching in the name of 'Life':

> In one of his first Socialist lectures, William Morris said: 'It is to stir you up *not* to be contented with a little that I am here tonight.' That is the job we have to do. If we wish to save people from the spreading taint of death, then we must win them for life. We do not wait for a new kind of person to appear until after Socialism has been won any more than we wait for Marxism to arise within a Communist society. We must change people *now*, for that is the essence of our cultural work. And in this work, all the forces of health within society are on our side: all those who, in whatever way, desire a richer life, all those who have warmer ambitions for Britain than those of tedious insolvency and re-armament, all those indeed, who desire any life at all, can be won to our side if we take to them the message of life against that of the slaughterhouse culture.[12]

Thompson's interest in Morris was, in the first place, a product of his literature teaching:

> I thought, how do I, first of all, raise with an adult class, many of them in the labour movement – discuss with them the significance of literature to their lives? And I started reading Morris. I was seized by Morris ... [13]

But it was also an example of the British Party's attempts in these years to rediscover and define a native, radical, cultural tradition. Jack Lindsay asked Thompson to write a fuller piece about Morris for *Arena*; it was too long, so Lindsay suggested he turn it into a booklet. Five years later, the 800 page 'booklet' was published by the Party's publishers, Lawrence and Wishart. *William Morris: Romantic to Revolutionary* was in many ways a 'Party book', generously acknowledging the help of Dona Torr, John Mahon, Maurice Cornforth (who had led the assault a few years earlier on Caudwell in the *Modern Quarterly*), Alick West (Chair of the Party's Writers' Group), Douglas Garman (then running the Party's Education Department) and Arnold Kettle, the last three of whom had read the book in manuscript. Quoting Tom Mann, A.L. Morton, Pollitt and Page Arnot (himself quoting Lenin), the book sought to rehabilitate Morris's early poetry – Sir Launcelot *versus* Mr Gradgrind, Mr Eliot and Mr Attlee – and to propose a rather different Morris to the one then invoked by the Labour Party:

> Morris, alas, despite all of Mr Attlee's incantations, would not have given his blessing to the 'Welfare State': when the 'ideal' was set before him of 'the capitalist public service ... brought to perfection', he merely remarked that he 'would not walk across the street for the realization of such an "ideal"'. Alas, again, he would not have rejoiced in the democratization of our blessed monarchy, he would not have stalked through the Malayan jungle with Mr Strachey in search of an enlightened imperialism, he would not have written Chants to our great American ally, he would not even have understood the new partnership of reformed capitalism and be-knighted labour in defence of the free world.[14]

In the late 1940s and early 1950s, then, there was no evident conflict between Thompson's membership of the Communist Party, his ideas about literature, or the teaching through which he expressed and developed them. Poetry, communism and adult education were three vectors of a busy working life of which the Morris book was simply the most sustained and successful expression.

❏ WEA or PBEA?

But the reviews of *William Morris* were not encouraging. By the early 1950s literature had become a key site of ideological conflict between (and within) the two blocs, one in which the 'West' had claimed the high moral ground by insisting – paradoxically, of course – that Literature was *not* ideological, an idea that quickly took root in adult education. And though it may have been a relatively quiet sector in the Cold War, adult education was not without its casualties.[15] So public a communist as Thompson knew that his politics made him vulnerable to charges of 'partiality'. Indeed, he felt that to pretend an easy-going 'impartiality' in his literature teaching was both dishonest and unlikely to inspire the kinds of discussion and argument he felt characterised the most successful adult classes. 'The class has always come alive', he wrote of his class in Halifax in 1959–60, 'vigorous, independent-minded, and often original.' For all its weaknesses, his class in Shepley in 1949–50 had 'one admirable characteristic which better classes lack':

'The students (mainly manual workers and housewives) show a sturdy independence, and maintain a kind of friendly aloofness towards the tutor – a confidence in their ability to make independent judgements and an eagerness to correct the tutor upon any matter upon which they feel themselves to be more expert.'

For Thompson, this kind of critical independence was connected with a belief in the wider resonance of the class and of his students' literary studies beyond the class; he felt confident that his Bingley students, for example, would 'continue their active and intelligent interest in literature', long after the class had finished, 'and exert a positive cultural influence within the community'. This belief clearly sustained his energies and enthusiasm through the frustrations of even the most disappointing classes. At the end of his first year in Shepley he wrote:

> It is the tutor's opinion that such classes as this should be both continued and encouraged. Certainly the class would benefit from an infusion of fresh blood and younger members. But, even as it is, it may be performing a more worth-while function than a class of far higher standards, confining its membership to the professional section of a large centre of population. In the latter case the result may only be to encourage an intellectual elite. At Shepley, a small industrial valley, it is necessary to grapple more realistically with problems of standards and popular culture. It is unlikely that the active trade-unionist will find in himself a specialist interest in problems of literary criticism or 'intellectual climate'. Must he therefore be denied an opportunity to gain acquaintance with major works of literature under qualified guidance? Even if the going is hard and the results unspectacular, this sort of class must be kept alive ...

This was not simply rhetoric, the kind of gesture that might be easier to make when writing a class report in the summer than on dark winter nights driving from Halifax over to Shepley. Thompson was making an argument here which his Director, Sidney Raybould, would have recognised. The previous year Raybould had published *University Standards in WEA Work*, followed in 1949 by *The Approach to WEA Teaching* and *The English Universities and Adult Education* in 1951, attempting to define – and therefore shape – the aims and character of university liberal adult education, and soon, by virtue of the force of his writing, acquiring the authority of orthodoxy in postwar, post-Butler Britain. At the heart of Raybould's vision for adult education was the notion of 'university standards'. This was partly a question of the intellectual level which the tutorial class should reach, at least by the third year. It was a level which – as Thompson admitted – his Shepley class was never going to reach. And although the class was permitted to continue, it was scarcely any less hard work for Thompson, and still a long way from Raybould's 'university standards'. This was a second year class, and yet three out of nine students did not complete any written work at all (one, who had no glasses, was forbidden by her doctor from even reading during the winter!); of the remaining six, two students submitted essays of less than 500 words. And yet, as Thompson argued, to neglect this kind of class would represent a betrayal of 'working class education' 'in favour of (an easier job for the tutor!) the further isolation of an elite'. He was particularly impressed by the intellectual effort that he knew was invested in 'the one contribution of a manual worker, over 60 years old':

> ... an essay of remarkable quality on *King Lear*, showing a most thorough knowledge of the play. This essay ... was the result of several evening's work, and of a great deal of thought and reading, re-reading and puzzling over difficult passages. The essay ... might be so much waste paper within a university's walls: the first page is a record of false starts and every phrase is marked with painful effort: but if every student had produced work of the same standard in relation to his training and abilities, the tutor would have held this up as an exemplary class.

If this was an implicit repudiation of Raybould's views of the role of the university in adult education, Thompson made it explicit the following year in a 10,000 word polemic *Against 'University' Standards*, where he characterised it as 'hostile to the healthy development of working-class adult education, a theory which would permit university domination to stifle the independent voluntary dynamic of the WEA'. For Thompson, 'the dynamic of the tutorial class movement' traditionally – and still, at best – derived, not from the university's intellectual 'standards' but from 'a fruitful conflict or interplay between the scholarship of the universities on the one hand, and the experience and social dynamic of the student on the other'. In particular, he ridiculed the idea that 'university standards' should seek the cultivation of a civilised 'tolerance' in the tutorial class as an end in itself:

> We may agree ... that the fostering of this disposition is a desirable by-product, without claiming it as an end or as an appropriate governing response to all situations of a certain kind. It may, indeed, be argued that there are other equally valuable by-products of the process, such as an increase in responsiveness to others, or of sensitivity, or of experience of democratic association, which some classes foster ... we must also bear in mind that, because we find a tolerant disposition or attitude on the whole desirable, there may be other dispositions or attitudes – compassionate, or militant, generous or spontaneous – equally desirable (or more appropriate) in certain circumstances. At the present moment, for instance, having just returned from a May Day meeting at which I was (without any kind of provocation) roughly ridden against and harried by mounted police, I am disposed to welcome a militant attitude on the part of the people in defence of traditional liberties ... [16]

His account of 'tolerance' as 'a typical form of class indoctrination' was a classical Marxist one, recognising that it was *of course* 'desirable for the ruling-class that the working-class should be tolerant in the face of injustice or exploitation':

> Education is not a self-contained process but a process within society. Man *acts* according to his experience. The more closely his experience (or knowledge, which is schematically ordered experience of a certain kind) approximates to reality, the more effective will his action be ... If the institutions of education are divorced from the sources of action, they will be re-organised. If a social class or grouping cannot permit the correction of error, because it defends their social position, then the society will become less efficient and decline, or they will be displaced from their dominant position by others.

The arguments of *Against 'University' Standards* were written in an embattled spirit (one which Thompson was to turn into a distinctive essay style of his own). They were an expression of the rapidly deteriorating intellectual climate of the Cold War – when a number of

Communist Party members lost their jobs in adult education, and many communist writers had difficulty publishing their work – a daring, unsupported guerrilla action in the 'Battle of Ideas'. In a world increasingly divided into two camps, it was, he argued, *impossible* 'in times of acute division – which are times of social, human, division for a man to be fully responsive to intolerable opinions'. Nevertheless, he felt sure that it was not in his literature classes that 'objectivity' was sacrificed most often to ideology:

> as a communist, I cannot fail to be aware that there exist terminal classes – indeed tutorials – in which little attempt is made – through the presentation of facts, the consideration of texts, and the dialectics of discussion – to give a fair presentation of views which are unpopular but exceedingly influential in their repercussions in the fields of Philosophy or International Relations or Economic Theory ...

'Seeing both sides of the question', 'objectivity', 'moderation' and 'tolerance' were, he felt, particular temptations for literature tutors, who too often encouraged a critical and intellectual numbness, inoculating students against both their own experiences and their reading, damaging their ability to respond to either the text or the world from which it came. 'I am aware of literature classes,' he wrote, in which 'the students are treated to "appreciations" and descriptive panegyrics'. On the other hand, he admitted his own sense of 'inadequacy and bias' when teaching 'certain uncongenial writers or the views of Catholic critics'. Literature teaching had a special responsibility in this divided world, not to disseminate 'culture' –

> I am reminded at once of one of those physical culture magazines, featuring naked torsos, all the muscle-attitudes fully developed – highly paid torsos suitable for exhibition wrestling bouts, a pride to their owners but precious little use to their fellow-men.

– but to draw attention to the conditions of language, its uses and misuses ('witness the degeneration of the BBC news service in the past five years, the increasing role of commentary, the calculated use of emotive words, the delicate manipulation of fact ...'). To those adult educators who disagreed, he suggested they should leave the WEA and use their devotion to 'university standards' to establish a BEA (Bourgeois Educational Association), or even a PBEA (Petty-Bourgeois Educational Association) ...

❑ Two fronts

Despite Thompson's strong sense of himself as a Communist Party member working inside adult education against the grain of Raybouldianism, the reading lists he gave his students were not obviously 'different' to those provided by other literature tutors in the Department, presumably reflecting the limitations of the book-boxes, as well as the expectations and enthusiasms of the class members with whom he negotiated the syllabus. The further reading suggested to members of his 1951–52 Bingley 'Aspects of Elizabethan Literature' class (which drew on his own Cambridge research interests), though more extensive than for any of his other courses, consisted largely of texts by Tillyard, Knights, Chambers, Boas, Dover Wilson, Willey, Wilson Knight, Travesi and even Bradley. Of course it is not the books in the book-box, but what you do with them that determines the success of a class; the most radical-looking reading-list is no guarantee of a radical – or an enjoyable – course. The third year of Thompson's Shepley class in 1950–51 studied 'Literature and Democracy', a literary version of the British Road to Socialism, beginning bravely with *Utopia*, *Henry IV Part 1* and Dekker's *Shoemaker's Holiday*, before moving through *Samson Agonistes*, *Gulliver's Travels*, Crabbe and Goldsmith, nineteenth-century working-class autobiography (Bamford, Cooper and Lovett), *Mary Barton* and *Past and Present*, before ending with 'the objective conditions of modern literature'. But meetings were soon down to an average of only five students, and Thompson felt in retrospect that the syllabus disguised (and encouraged) 'a complete inability to maintain any close or disciplined attention to the work in hand'. On the other hand, while he may have enjoyed the resistance of his Cleckheaton students in 1950–51 to mainstream critical opinion (particularly regarding the hateful Eliot) watching the class yawn cannot have brought him much satisfaction. There is little pleasure in repeatedly teaching texts only to demonstrate a negative point.

The further reading suggested for his Bingley course in 1949–50 did include two books of Marxist criticism, Caudwell's *Illusion and Reality* and Ralph Fox's *The Novel and the People*. But among three titles by Richards (*Principles of Literary Criticism*, *Science and Poetry* and *Practical Criticism*), two by Day Lewis (*The Poetic Image* and *Poetry and You*), two from the Leavises (*Fiction and the Reading Public* and *The Great Tradition*), Forster's *Aspects of the Novel* and David Cecil's *Early Victorian Novelists*, they must have looked, particularly in a preparatory year, distinctly vulnerable, rare and rapidly obsolete products of a stunted tradition of native Marxist literary criticism.

For what other Marxist critical texts could he have included? The writings of Gramsci, Benjamin and Bakhtin were then unknown in Britain, Brecht was known only as a dramatist, and Lukacs' *Studies in European Realism* was not published in English until that year. Alick West's *Crisis in Criticism* had been out of print since the late 1930s, while both Jack Lindsay and George Thomson were increasingly identified with the hardening Cold War cultural orthodoxies of King Street. The seriousness of this critical vacuum (and of course much else) was manifest when that year Lawrence and Wishart published *On Literature, Music and Philosophy* by that 'outstanding Marxist theoretician' A.A. Zhdanov. The damage to what remained of the Communist Party's cultural energies was dramatic, including a hasty attempt to limit the reputation of Caudwell's recently republished *Illusion and Reality*. Thompson was increasingly conscious of the weakness of existing Marxist aesthetics and of the self-defeating philistinism of the Party's cultural life in the early 1950s. *Our Time* had folded in 1949, *Circus* in 1950 and the eclectic *Arena* effectively closed in 1951 (after Lindsay and Swingler were instructed by the Party's National Cultural Committee to turn it into a 'fighting journal of socialist realism'[17]). For all the exhortations of Emile Burns and the NCC, the Party had signally failed (and so, as he bitterly knew, had Edward Thompson) to begin to produce a native, Socialist, imaginative literature. Instead the NCC had committed the Party to a reductive and mechanical model of culture imported from the Soviet Union, marginalised its most distinguished writers (like Swingler and Rickword) in favour of sentimental sloganising poets like Oscar Thomson and Stella Jackson, and presided over the failure of all its literary publications only to re-invent a kind of heavy handed Third Period workerist culture with the short-lived *Daylight*. Although Thompson was dismayed by the proposal, he was reassured that the magazine was to be edited by Margot Heinemann, and he submitted a poem to the first issue, 'Trafalgar Square 1951', invoking a vision of the working masses on the march from Mile End to Leningrad.[18]

Daylight was a clumsy attempt to marginalise those poets around Fore Publications (Swingler, Rickword and Lindsay) who had been identified with all the Party's literary publications since the early 1930s. It was a product of what Thompson then called 'Emilism' (after Emile Burns) an economistic and bureaucratic suspicion of the imagination which he felt continually sabotaged the Party's cultural efforts. He was now too busy writing *William Morris* to help Swingler fight Burns or to find much time for writing verse. But in many ways 'Emilism' was the 'real' subject of *William Morris*. For it was a Party book in another, rather different sense. Written 'on two fronts', against those critics who minimised or decried Morris' communism, and against those Marxists who minimised or decried the validity of the imagination, it was a coded attempt to re-invigorate English Marxist criticism by invoking a utopian, creative and moral view of poetry. Desire *versus* Necessity, against Mr Burns and Mr Stalin as much as Mr Attlee, poetry against the mechanistic dogma of Party orthodoxy.

It was during the five years he was working on *William Morris* (between 1951 and 1955) that Thompson's teaching programme began to shift towards classes in history and away from literature – two classes in social history in 1951–52, three in both 1952–53 and 1953–54, rising to four in 1954–55; apart from the fourth year of his Batley class in 1951–52, the only literature classes he taught in these years were in Bingley (where he taught from 1948–53), Middlesbrough (from 1953–56) and the third year of a class at Leeds in 1953–54. As he explained to Swingler, teaching and writing history did not bring him into conflict with the Party in the way that writing literary criticism and poetry increasingly did.

Considering the importance the Communist Party placed upon literature as a front in the 'Battle of Ideas', it is perhaps surprising how rarely Thompson seems to have included contemporary writing in his courses. But there were disheartening defeats on that front too. 'If this year's work has not been quite so pleasing as last year's,' he wrote of his Batley class in 1952–53, 'it is because contemporary literature is pitiful stuff compared with Shakespeare'. No twentieth-century poet appeared more often than Yeats (usually contrasted with Eliot). The only postwar novels that regularly appeared on his reading-lists were Graham Greene's *The Heart of the Matter* (the key text then in the Party's demonisation of Greene) and by way of contrast, Joyce Cary's anti-imperialist *Mister Johnson* (significantly Orwell never appeared).

Thompson was continually dismayed by the resistance of classes to reading contemporary texts on the syllabus. In Shepley in 1949–50 he had been particularly disappointed by his students' response to *The Grapes of Wrath*; 'it appeared that the capacity of the students for making judgements on literary worth diminished in proportion to the contemporary nature of the work and the issues treated,' adding, 'but this weakness is not confined to WEA students !' Eight weeks on 'Literature and Politics in the Thirties' in the fourth year of the Bingley class in 1953–54 gave him a rare – and brief – opportunity to introduce members of the class to some rather more radical writers like Sholokov, Malraux, O'Casey, Steinbeck, Silone, Dos Passos, Gorki and Upton Sinclair. But there are limits to the books that even the most inspiring of tutors can persuade their students to enjoy. In Cleckheaton in 1950–51 Thompson reported a difficult and frustrating year, even the best students 'polite but indifferent spectators', that is until they read *The Star Turns Red*. At this point the class 'touched rock bottom', suddenly 'united in their judgement that (however admirable O'Casey's intentions and experimentation might be) the mouthfuls of assorted rhetoric, symbolism and naturalism would not come to life'.

❑ Too little rebellion

At least this class argued back. Thompson's most repeatedly expressed disappointment was with literature classes stuck in a 'rather comfortable rut'. Though in Middlesbrough he could report with satisfaction that the class had undertaken a great deal of reading, he felt that no really searching discussions or questions seem to have come forward. The reluctance of students to enter into critical argument about the books they were reading, was the source of a continuing and mounting frustration with his literature teaching, the kind of students he referred to as 'I know what I like', 'anyone is as good as anyone' and 'you tutors are always reading things into the books'. 'There is too little rebellion in the class,' he said of Bingley in 1951–52,

> and they are too content to be *taught*. It looks as if the whole course of the class might be run without one good earnest row between the students, and perhaps provocative methods will have to be taken in the final year (mainly in contemporary literature) to remind them that the study of literature can sting as well as soothe.

At the end of his first three year tutorial in Batley he felt that 'the most serious criticism of the group is that they still appear really in need of a tutor to help them read, criticise and think, and do not have the self-confidence and independence to strike out on their own'. And experience is no guarantee of success. Six years later Thompson found himself teaching another class in Batley, one which 'defied all attempts to unify it and to bring all members into participation':

> Ages have ranged from 18 to 80: romantic non-conformity, post war couldn't-care-less-ism, and nineteenth century ultra-rationalism have grated against each other and refused to find points of contact. Whatever method the tutor has tried exercises, analysis of poetry, the solid straight from the shoulder hour lecture, even the reading of one of Sheridan's plays to try to make the atmosphere chummy – there has always been some dissident section ostentatiously refusing to 'come in'.[19]

By the end of 1959 there were only six students left of an initial enrolment of sixteen:

> The morale of the survivors ultimately declines. The morale of the tutor declines too, as he becomes aware of the way in which the sense of duty, and of personal obligation to himself, brings the loyal core to the class each week, rather than the satisfactions of the work itself. Teaching under these conditions can become very difficult.

By this date, of course, covert resistance to 'Emilism' had become an open fight against its greater and more deadly sponsor, Stalinism. Arguments begun inside the Communist Party had become arguments against it and outside it. It may not be a coincidence that after 1956 Thompson again began teaching more classes in literature than in history. But if literature was no longer a site of political conflict for Thompson, it was a source of other frustrations. His new political responsibilities – notably the *New Reasoner* – kept him from writing the poetry he wanted to write just as much as Communist Party activity ever had. Moreover his Class Reports record a deepening dissatisfaction with his literature teaching, with the ways in which literature as an adult education subject seemed to be turning into a retreat from the contemporary world, not a point of entry or of engagement with it. For the student population was changing. The students in his Batley class in 1956–57 were younger and more middle class than in previous classes there, better read but lacking, he regretted to say, 'the same earnest purposeful approach of the older tutorial students':

> Intelligent, sophisticated, immature in their outlook (it is interesting to find that these young teachers who have themselves been taught in a Leavis-influenced tradition, have built-in responses

antipathetic to all things 'romantic' including Blake, Wordsworth, Shelley, Keats, etc) and a little superior. ... A generation influenced by Kingsley Amis and St Colin Wilson will take some assimilating.

Thompson made his own feelings clear about the *trahison des clercs* of the late 1950s in 'Outside the Whale', a long polemic against Natopolis that traced the culture of the Bomb back through Amis and the Movement to Eliot, Auden and Orwell:

> There are no good causes left, not because of any lack of causes, but because within Natopolitan culture the very notion of a good cause is an embarrassment. ... In Natopolitan culture today, no swearword is more devastating than 'romantic'. ... It was left to Mr Amis to make the ultimate definition of political romanticism: 'an irrational capacity to become inflamed by interests and causes that are not one's own, that are outside oneself'. ... Self-interest is not only comfortable: it is also wholesome and sane and does not make revolutions.[20]

In this culture of 'tired disenchantment' he found discussions with his students constantly slipping away from literature into other vocabularies, as in Morley in 1959–60:

> An attempt to introduce some post-war writing was only partially successful. The bad language in *Roots* horrified several of the adult school people, and disabled them from discussing anything else: *The Lord of the Flies* provoked more sustained attention, although it tended towards the merits and demerits of CND.

Worse, students in literature classes seemed increasingly to regard reading as a source of entertainment rather than an object of study (still less a tool of social criticism). If 'knitting and a tea interval' set the tone of his first Ossett class, eleven years later in Morley it was still 'hard going', as he struggled against 'a sense of philistinism pushed back towards the walls but likely to press back in at the least opportunity, a tendency to hang social or even local gossip on some literary peg and run away with irrelevancies in discussion'. When he began teaching in Harrogate in 1959–60, he found a class of 28 students, many of whom had 'no experience of sustained study, and with the expectation of attending a series of lectures – at "university level" – which would combine the functions of intellectual stimulation and of a social occasion', and who voiced considerable opposition to written work and class exercises:

> I decided to adopt a tougher policy than I would have dared at the usual class: actively to discourage the more dilettante students by setting standards high from the start, by selecting fairly difficult texts, and by dispensing almost altogether with lectures in favour of close textual discussion.

The result, he was pleased to report, was a dramatic fall in the register to 13 students, and on the sixth evening, a class mutiny:

> It is possible I carried this policy too far: and on one evening ... when I was slogging hard at an exercise taken from a contemporary newspaper, there was something like a rebellion from several class members who exclaimed indignantly that this was not what they had expected of a literature course.

While Thompson did not recommend this approach for more 'traditional' classes (i.e. in the West Riding), it obviously worked well in Harrogate, resulting in 'a first-rate class which in the second half of the year it has been a pleasure to teach'. Two years later it was still 'a delightful class to teach,' since 'there has been no need to push it at any point. The students have read widely enough to keep the tutor on his toes. ... There were few class meetings in which the tutor did not find himself being taught.'

But this was PBEA territory, hardly the vision of literature as a 'stirring-up' against contentment or a weapon in the struggle against the charnel-house culture. And the pleasures of teaching Hopkins's poetry in Harrogate could not compare with the satisfactions of teaching courses in social history out of which was to emerge the research for a new book. One of the first of those courses, in Batley, also began with a student rebellion, when survivors of the previous year's literature class left in protest because they were expected to study nineteenth-century literature *and social history*. As a result, Thompson found himself left with a class which he said, 'began to show signs of becoming what I had once dreamed a tutorial class in industrial Yorkshire could be like – but which I had never before begun to experience ...'. By 1963, the year the book was published as *The Making of the English Working Class*, he was teaching three classes in social history and only one in literature. Two years later Thompson left Leeds for

Warwick, his arguments with literature, communism and adult education apparently over.

❏ Handing on

After he had left Leeds, however, Thompson repeatedly returned to literary subjects – essays on Wordsworth and Coleridge, Blake. Caudwell, Morris, and the American poet Tom McGrath; the substantially re-written *William Morris*; two poetry pamphlets, *Homage to Salvador Allende* and *Infant and Emperor*, the long poem, 'Powers and Names' and the Swiftian novel *The Sykaos Papers*; a study of his father's relationship with the Bengali poet Tagore, an edition of poems by Mary Collier and Stephen Duck, and the much-delayed study of Blake. Literature, in particular poetry and poetry-criticism, clearly remained sites of pleasure, engagement and conflict for Thompson all his life, providing a special kind of utterance to which he returned again and again up to the last page of barely-veiled autobiography in *Witness Against the Beast*:

> His vision had been not into the rational government *of* man, but into the liberation of an unrealised potential, an alternative nature, within man: a nature masked by circumstance, repressed by the Moral Law ... it was the intensity of this vision, which derived from sources far older than the Enlightenment, which made it impossible for Blake to fall into the courses of apostasy. When ... the revolutionary fires burned low in the early 1800s, Blake had his own way of 'keeping the divine vision in time of trouble'. This way had been prepared long before by the Ranters and the Diggers in their defeat, who had retired from activist strife to Gerard Winstanley's 'kingdom within, which moth and rust doth not corrupt'. And so Blake also took the characteristic antinomian retreat into more esoteric ways, handing on to the initiates 'The Everlasting Gospel'. There is obscurity and perhaps even some oddity in this. But there is never the least sign of any submission to 'Satan's Kingdom'.[21]

'Satan's Kingdom' took many guises in Thompson's lifetime, and his refusal to submit to its laws took different forms. The poetic imagination was one of the most enduring of these – an arena of confrontation, a tool of social criticism, a badge of commitment, an expression of dissent, a defensive line, a bridgehead of cultural challenge, a special kind of code, a moral talisman, an infinitely powerful form of rhetoric, a place of retreat, and the source of a vision of the future that was always political but which also spoke against politics and beyond it. Among the many continuing arguments that defined a life of vigorous argument, his arguments on behalf of the literary imagination and his arguments within and against it remained at the centre of his vision. And those arguments he began while he was at Leeds. To be more specific, they were crucially shaped by his experience of teaching literature at Leeds; not only in adult education, but in the tutorial class movement; not only as a tutor for the WEA, but as a communist; and not only as a communist but as one who was active in the debates and disputes about literature inside the Communist Party. Long after he had taken those arguments elsewhere they were still recognisably the arguments he had begun in his years at Leeds, first on behalf of adult education, communism and literature, later by arguments with them.

Andy Croft is a tutor in the Leeds University Adult Education Centre and has written extensively on the CPGB and culture.

NOTES

All the quotations from Thompson's Class Reports and Syllabus are from papers held in the Archive of the Department of Adult Continuing Education, University of Leeds. I wish to record my thanks to Tom Steele for his help in making these available.

I also wish to thank Dorothy Thompson for her encouraging and helpful comments on an earlier draft. Originally it contained quotations from the extensive surviving correspondence between Thompson and Randall Swingler, and from Thompson's published poetry; I have however respected Dorothy Thompson's request not to quote from letters or the poems until they are published, although I am conscious that in parts the piece seems therefore to rely on unsupported assertions. I wish to record my thanks to Judy Williams and Dorothy Thompson for permission to use the quotation in the epigraph.

1. See for example, Lin Chun, *The British New Left* (1993); Bryan Palmer, *E.P. Thompson: Objections and Oppositions* (1994) and Michael Kenny, *The First New Left: British Intellectuals After Stalin* (1995).
2. For a general account of Thompson's teaching at Leeds see Peter Searby, John Rule and Robert Malcolmson, 'Edward Thompson as a Teacher: Yorkshire and Warwick' in John Rule and Robert Malcolmson, *Protest and*

Survival: the Historical Experience (1993), where the testimony of surving students puts into perspective Thompson's sometimes rather self-lacerating accounts of his teaching. See also David Goodway, 'E.P. Thompson and the Making of *The Making of the English Working Class*' in Richard Taylor (ed.) *Beyond the Walls: Fifty Years of Adult and Continuing Education at the University of Leeds, 1946–1996* (1995). See also John Goode, 'E. P Thompson and "the Significance of Literature"' in Harvey J. Kaye and Keith McClelland (eds) *E.P. Thompson: Critical Perspectives* (1990) and H. Abelove, in *History and Theory*, 21 (1982).

3. 'An Interview with E P Thompson', *Radical History Review*, 3 (Fall 1976).

4. For the Communist Party Writers' Group and *Our Time*, see Andy Croft, 'Writers, the Communist Party and the Battle of Ideas' in *Socialist History*, no. 5 (1994).

5. The phrase is Thompson's, from a review of Hamish Henderson's *Elegies for the Dead in Cyrenica* in *Our Time*, June 1949; see 'New Year, 1948' *Our Time*, August 1948.

6. The importance of this incident for Lindsay may be indicated by the fact that he recounted it in three separate books – in *Meetings with Poets* (1968), *The Crisis in Marxism* (1981) and *Life Rarely Tells* (1982).

7. See E.P. Thompson, 'Edgell Rickword', *PN Review*, supplement xxviii, vol. 6 no. 1, 1979; see also Charles Hobday, *Edgell Rickword: A Poet at War* (1981).

8. 'The Place Called Choice', published in E.P. Thompson, *The Heavy Dancers* (1985); for the Festival of Britain poetry competition, see Andy Croft, 'Betrayed Spring: the 1945 Labour Government and British Literary Culture' in Jim Fyrth (ed.) *Labour's Promised Land?: Culture and Society in Labour Britain, 1945–51* (1995).

9. 'On the Liberation of Seoul', *Arena* 2 (6), February/March 1951; for *Arena* see Laurence Coupe, 'Jack Lindsay, From the Aphrodite to Arena' in Bob Mackie (ed.) *Jack Lindsay: the Thirties and Forties* (1984) and Andy Croft, 'Authors take Sides: Writers and the Communist Party, 1920–56' in Geoff Andrews, Nina Fishman and Kevin Morgan (eds) *Opening the Books: Essays on the Social and Cultural History of the British Communist Party* (Pluto Press, 1995).

10. 'Guest Notebook', *Daily Worker*, 12 June 1952.

11. E.P. Thompson, *The Struggle for a Free Press* (1952) p. 23; Thompson was also planning to write a series of historical pamphlets for the Party in time for the coronation.

12. E.P. Thompson, 'William Morris and the Moral Issues of Today' *Arena* 2 (8), June/July 1951, special issue; 'The Murder of William Morris' appeared

in *Arena* 2 (8), June/July 1951; Thompson also lectured on Morris to the Leeds Communist Party forum (*Daily Worker* 14 October 1950).
13. 'An Interview with E.P. Thompson', *Radical History Review*.
14. E.P. Thompson, *William Morris: Romantic to Revolutionary* (1955), p. 841.
15. See Roger Fieldhouse, *Adult Education and the Cold War* (Leeds Studies in Adult and Continuing Education, 1985).
16. *Against 'University Standards': Comments Upon the Reflections of Messrs Baxendall, Shaw and Mcleish*, Leeds University Adult Education papers vol. 1 no. 4 (July 1950)
17. For Thompson's later reflections on the Caudwell controversy (which he did not join) see E.P. Thompson, 'Caudwell', *Socialist Register*, 1977, particularly his comments on the 'Jungle Marxism' of King Street; in 1950 Thompson did join the correspondence in the *Daily Worker* about the 'Key Poets' series, defending Swingler and Lindsay from the 'self-righteous abuse' of Stella Jackson and others.
18. 'Trafalgar Square', *Daylight*, vol. 1 no. 1, Autumn 1952. For *Daylight* and the Communist Party's literary life in these years see Andy Croft, 'The End of Socialist Realism: Margot Heinemann's *The Adventurers*' in Mary Joannou and David Margolies (eds) *Heart of a Heartless World: Essays on Culture and Commitment in Honour of Margot Heinemann* (Pluto Press, 1995).
19. Dorothy Thompson remembers her husband's amazement at the level of discussion in her classes; 'We decided it was because I was a woman, younger than most of the class, not very authoritative in my status, that they were prepared to wade in and criticise and also to volunteer their own judgements. He was very envious, but I think the point was that he was impressive as a speaker ... so that discussion in his classes was much more inhibited.' (letter to the author, 10 August 1994).
20. E.P. Thompson, 'Outside the Whale' in E.P. Thompson (ed.) (1960); republished in E.P. Thompson, *The Poverty of Theory* (1979), pp. 13, 20.
21. E.P. Thompson, *Witness Against the Beast: William Blake and the Moral Law* (1993), p. 229.

TOWARDS A BIOGRAPHY OF E.P. THOMPSON

Harvey J. Kaye

LIKE MANY OF MY colleagues, I wondered who would be granted the official endorsement to write Edward Thompson's biography. In the course of a long evening chat with Dorothy Thompson (and Sheila Rowbotham) at a conference on Edward's life and work held at Stanford University in January 1994, I asked her that very question. Dorothy's answer was that she would not be granting access to Edward's papers for such a project so long as the British and other governments kept their own files on Edward closed. However, she added that she welcomed the writing of intellectual biographies.

Bryan Palmer's *E.P. Thompson: Objections and Oppositions* (Verso, 1994) will likely be recognised as the first of such intellectual biographies – even though Palmer makes it very clear at the outset that his book was not written as such. And truly, while biographical in form, the work reads, as Palmer intended it to, like a long, well-researched essay of remembrance and appreciation by a younger scholar who, having first admired Edward from afar through his writings and politics, came to know him personally through correspondence, visits and a short period of colleagueship and in the process grew to like and admire him all the more.

Bryan Palmer is a professor of history at Queens University, Ontario. An accomplished labour historian and energetic promoter of labour and left historiography in Canada, he first wrote about Thompson in *The Making of E.P. Thompson: Marxism, Humanism and History* (1981). More recently, he authored *Descent Into Discourse: The Reification of Language and the Writing of Social History* (1990), offering a welcome and critical examination of the spread of postmodernist and poststructuralist thought in historical studies.

To be honest, Palmer and I have had an uneven relationship. I am willing to consider the possibility that it has been due – whatever our actual intentions – to a sense of competition over 'representing' E.P. Thompson. It is unfortunate because on most of the fundamental issues we seem to be in agreement, and this holds true for most of the points he makes in his new book. At the same time, I remain fascinated by Palmer's proprietorial attitude. For example: I am not sure who he has in mind when he makes such remarks, but in the course of 'An

Interview with Bryan D. Palmer: Historicizing E.P. Thompson', he comments: 'whatever its many shortcomings [*The Making of E.P. Thompson*] covered ground in a political way that others have been reproducing in the service of their academic careers for the last ten years'.[1] Moreover, in the book Palmer talks somewhat dismissively about the innumerable commentaries which have appeared on Thompson as an 'industry', and yet, he has now written two books, a number of articles and even allowed himself to be interviewed on the man.

As I said, I am essentially in agreement with the points Palmer makes in the new book, and I must definitely compliment him on certain notable features of the work. Following the Preface and Introduction, his first chapter discusses at greater length than any previous study of E.P. Thompson, the work and words of E.P.'s father, Edward John Thompson, and how they likely shaped E.P.'s own life and career. Palmer rightly emphasises the influence which Edward senior assuredly had upon his younger son and, in particular, this leads him to highlight E.P. Thompson's 'internationalism'.

This is a really important point – one which Palmer smartly makes against the persistent arguments of many British historians and cultural studies scholars, the latter of which, ever since the exciting days of the Birmingham University Centre for Contemporary Cultural Studies, have regularly portrayed Thompson as merely an English nationalist, practically a 'little Englander'. Indeed, I sat in sessions at the summer 1994 History Workshop conference (London), held in memory of Thompson, and heard descriptions of the man that I found astounding. Apparently ignoring Thompson's ties to, and writings on, India, his many friends and activities in North America and his leadership role in European and international nuclear disarmament campaigns, certain speakers described Edward as if he was secluded in his Worcestershire home at Wick Episcopi like some gentry figure and writing nothing more than tracts in defence of *English* history and culture against any and all foreign influences. Therefore, as an antidote to such nonsense, I heartily endorse Palmer's insistent portrait of Thompson the internationalist.

But, of course, Thompson was both an internationalist and a nationalist. As Palmer ably demonstrates, Thompson was an internationalist in that he was possessed of an internationalism engendered by his upbringing, his personal experiences both in the war against fascism and in postwar reconstruction efforts in the Balkans, and his

TOWARDS A BIOGRAPHY OF E.P. THOMPSON 51

continuing multinational solidarities and endeavours. And yet, there can be no denying his nationalism, derived from a particular reading of English and British history and, again, his own experience and engagements. In short, Thompson's class-structure-and-struggle understanding of history enabled him to appreciate more than most that many of the finest features of modern English and British history were determined by popular struggles from below. He took seriously the tradition of the 'free-born Briton'.

While I welcome Palmer's assertion of Thompson's internationalism, I am disappointed by his tendency in this book to portray Thompson the historian, the critic and the activist as essentially a loner. In doing so, he seems to consign Edward to the same internal exile at Wick Episcopi that the cultural-studies folk do.

❏ The Historians' Group

Palmer all but ignores Thompson's own intellectual and historiographical formation in the Communist Party Historians' Group. Although Dorothy was more regularly engaged in its activities, nevertheless, Edward himself fully acknowledged the influence of the Historians' Group (1946–56). Regarding becoming a historian, Edward said in 1976:

> I got this fascination with the archives. I suppose this plus the critical, comradely help of one or two people in particular, especially Dona Torr, and participation in the Communist Party Historians' Group, in which we had theoretical discussions all the time – this made me into a historian. The formal and informal exchange with fellow socialists helped me more than anything. ... Socialist intellectuals ought to help each other. We should never be wholly dependent upon institutions, however benevolent, but should maintain groups in which theory is discussed and history is discussed and in which people criticise each other. This principle of being able to give and receive sharp criticism is very important.[2]

I note the Historians' Group not just because of its formative influence on Thompson, but also because Palmer does not give due credit to the pioneering work accomplished by its other (former) members which, again, Edward himself acknowledged *and* critically appreciated as the foundations for his own studies. I am thinking here of George Rudé's prior and original explorations of eighteenth-century England

and the urban crowd (not noted at all by Palmer), and the other histories 'from the bottom up' pursued by Rodney Hilton, Christopher Hill and Eric Hobsbawm among others – who themselves learned a great deal from Thompson. Furthermore (and Palmer writes only a little on this), Thompson recorded how he saw himself standing within a particular Marxist 'tradition' which went back to Marx himself, was enriched by William Morris and included his comrades in the Group, as well as the editors of the *Socialist Register*, John Saville and Ralph Miliband (the former of whom was a central figure in the Group).

❏ Links and friendships

Of course, Edward Thompson, like anyone involved in the inevitable solititude of scholarship and the seemingly incessant traumas of the politics of the left, had his moments of isolation, loneliness and crankiness (and, fortunately, more than most he knew how to turn those feelings to dramatic literary ends). But, contrary to the picture of Edward Thompson as a loner, I think of him in terms of the many people and movements with whom he worked and campaigned; the many students he taught, encouraged and learned from, both in adult education classes and more traditional academic settings on both sides of the Atlantic; and his many friends including those in North America like C. Wright Mills, Tom McGrath, David Montgomery, Herbert Gutman (and the much younger Bryan Palmer himself) – which is not even to mention the many friends and acquaintances from around the globe who were regularly entertained at Wick Episcopi. I am sure that Palmer would agree with this, but it is not adequately portrayed in his new book.

Aside from this, Bryan Palmer is to be commended. He has written a good remembrance and a deeply sincere and warm appreciation of Edward Thompson's career as radical scholar and political dissenter.

I have one more observation. Palmer refers to Thompson's Herbert Gutman Memorial Lecture of April 1988 dealing with the Brothertown (or Brotherton) Indians who started out in the New York area in the eighteenth century. He adds how 'After that lecture, Edward, Dorothy and I drove north, through upstate New York, visiting Brothertown, where Occum's people eventually settled.' I can readily appreciate that drive, for the story continues in the midwest. When Edward visited my family and me in Green Bay, Wisconsin in spring 1990, to speak to my students and colleagues, he delivered again his

Gutman Memorial Lecture. It was a wonderful occasion. As I recollect him explaining, the subject was something he came upon when the wrong set of papers were placed before him at the London Library. The documents treated the actual origins of the Brotherton Indians. Apparently 'formed' in the late eighteenth century by English missionaries seeking to protect the remnants of various New England tribes, the Brotherton developed their own collective identity and later removed themselves to Wisconsin, establishing the new town of Brotherton on the eastern shore of Lake Winnebago (about the same time in the early nineteenth century that a large segment of the Oneida Nation moved out here from New York).

Although Edward was not in the greatest health, he fully rose to the occasion and spoke excitedly and passionately for more than an hour. As Green Bay is not so very far north of where the Brotherton had settled in Wisconsin, Edward was eager to visit the area the next day and my family and I were pleased to oblige. On the way we stopped at antique and secondhand shops, for Edward was hoping to find evidence of, and references to, the Brotherton settlement. More rewardingly, when we stopped to ask for directions, Edward proceeded to amaze me by turning each stop into an oral history session – the locals we met immediately sensed he was to be trusted. With help, we found our way to the original Brotherton cemetery, barely marked, but not far off the main road. Edward was thrilled by the discovery and he and our two young daughters, aged ten and six, went from headstone to headstone surveying the names, dates and other engraved information still legible. Their first experience as historians, Rhiannon and Fiona that day apprenticed themselves to *the* master craftsman.

Harvey J. Kaye is the Rosenberg Professor of Social Change and Development at the University of Wisconsin-Green Bay and the author of The British Marxist Historians *(1984),* The Powers of the Past *(1991),* The Education of Desire: Marxists and the Writing of History *(1992), and* 'Why Do Ruling Classes Fear History?' and Other Questions *(1996).*

NOTES

1. *Left History*, fall 1993.
2. Abelove, H., et al, *Visions of History* (MAHRO, 1983).

ERIC HOBSBAWM: A HISTORIAN LIVING THROUGH HISTORY

What follows is an edited transcript of an interview with Eric Hobsbawm first broadcast on BBC Radio Three's 'Night Waves' on 1 November 1994, where he reflects on the issues raised in his book, *Age Of Extremes*. Socialist History is grateful to Eric Hobsbawm and the BBC for giving permission for us to print it.

What are the difficulties of writing a history of your own age?

The usual things: that you are too close to it; that you find it very difficult to distinguish from your actions and opinions at the time. On the other hand there are two ways in which historians are in a better position to do it: one, we now know a particular period has ended and so to that extent we can slightly stand outside it; and second, that the basic thing about history is precisely that you take your distance. You try, or at least the kind of historian I am, tries to stand at a point where you can see the whole thing. So to that extent historians are natural correctors of the close focus vision which the media – and for that matter people who simply live through day by day or year by year – necessarily have on affairs, including their own lifetime.

Do you then have to cultivate that sense of detachment in a rather different way when writing about a period you've lived through than you would say about the nineteenth century, which you've also obviously written about?

In the nineteenth century everything that comes to you is, as it were, at secondhand. Today, if you write about your own lifetime you are writing about something in which you are emotionally involved. There is an intermediate period about which I've tried to write in one of my books which is neither the one nor the other. But there are, of course, advantages of writing about your own lifetime: you know what it felt like, you know what it was like, which is in some sense important, even though it does not actually help you to get the facts straight. It gives you a way of judging particularly what younger historians who write at secondhand feel about this. I had exactly the same experience in my first research when I was precisely researching on something which some very old gentlemen who were still around could remember; they said, 'This is very interesting and I'm sure you know more about it than I do and can remember, but it actually wasn't quite like that.'

You do choose to insert yourself in an almost autobiographical way at certain moments in Age Of Extremes. *Are those very considered moments when you feel the need to use the first person singular?*

Not really. It happens that there are, I mean, some bits and pieces with which I have had direct connections: well, it seems natural, for instance, at the moment when Hitler came to power in Germany; it happens to be a biographical moment, which makes a historical moment, if you like, more vivid for other people.

To what extent, do you think, now you've looked at this short century, that the October Revolution of 1917 is in fact the axis on which everything that follows up until our present time turns?

I try and present it in a slightly more general way. The axis is the collapse of the liberal bourgeois society of the nineteenth century. I see the October Revolution as an aspect of this collapse and because of the depth of this collapse in the 30 years or so after 1914 it played an enormous role, a central role, and because in a sense liberal society and liberal capitalism could only be saved as liberal capitalism, as distinct from fascist capitalism or authoritarian capitalism, through the intervention of the Soviet Union and the Red Army, thereby creating a superpower in Moscow, clearly the role of the October Revolution and the state it created is central, and I suppose, if you like in the simplest way, the period I write about is a period from the October Revolution, give or take a year or two, to the end of the Soviet Union, give or take a year or two.

If the achievement of the revolution, and its successors Stalin and the period of Soviet communism, is to have compelled capitalism to have reformed itself, does that then become the justification, do you think, for Stalin and, perhaps, for the appalling things, which you admit are appalling, that happened in the Soviet Union from the late-twenties up until the coming of the Second World War?

It's not my business to justify the Soviet Union or Stalin or anything. I'm trying to write the history of the short twentieth century.

You write early on in your introduction that one can see the history of this short twentieth century as a series of wars of religion. I suppose one thinks inevitably of the Thirty Years' War, and one thinks of other periods in the sixteenth and seventeenth centuries when wars of religion had been dominant. You really do see the conflict between capitalism and communism as almost a theological battle?

I see it being waged in theological terms. In actual fact there was no war between capitalism and communism: there were wars between capitalist countries; there were wars between communist countries; there was actually no war between capitalism and communism. What there was was a war of theologians backed by military-industrial complexes which found theology very useful.

To what extent do you argue, do you think, that the victims of this war of theologians in the end are those countries in the Third and developing world, be they under the aegis of Soviet communism or be they supported and enhanced by the United States and liberal capitalism?

Well, clearly the victims in the second half of the century were those countries in which the United States thought it actually had to fight the war, hot war, Vietnam and all these other places. Otherwise, I would have thought, the major victims, one of the big victims, in the whole thing, was the Russian people, the great victim people of the twentieth century, never mind what the ideologies and the regimes under which it has been governed are, they are the ones that had really the bad end of things and continue to have the bad ends; and we are the ones that have benefited indirectly or directly from their sufferings.

How would you seek, as a historian, to explain the eventual collapse of the Soviet Union?

I try and make this point: I think this was the only way in which a very backward country, in which no conditions for the development of socialism were present, could have gone, by a forced race to rapid industrialisation and modernisation. This was undertaken by a system which was also not qualified to undertake this because they simply had not the infrastructure or, for that matter, the cadres to do it; and consequently, while they had great achievements, these great achievements were limited and moreover what they could lead to is ... effectively it was bound to run down. The major achievements were the achievements of war economies and when these achievements had been actually obtained there was no long-term future. They could have gone on for a very long time; they were not collapsing, but it was not competitive, internationally competitive. Paradoxically, it was the West which was much better at planning once it had learnt that it had to. Now, of course, Western governments can decide to forget about it again, though Western corporations don't.

It is often argued that with the collapse of Soviet communism and the various countries who followed in its model that somehow Marxism as a system of thought is invalidated. Do you feel as an historian, a Marxist historian, that nonetheless it remains an important and valuable methodology for the historian, a tool of investigation that only a fool would throw out with the failure of the Soviet Union?

Actually only fools do throw it out. The great bulk of historians have absorbed far more of the Marxist approach to history than was ever conceived possible in the days when I was a student. Whether they call themselves Marxist or whether they don't call themselves Marxist is, if you like, an autobiographical question. I personally don't mind people saying 'Are you a Marxist?' I am because I owe an enormous amount to this, but about the usefulness of the Marxist approach to history there can be, in my view, no doubt at all.

What do you think are the particular aspects of Marxism that historians who wouldn't call themselves Marxist have absorbed and bring into play in their historical writing?

The essential connection, as it were, the order of priorities, that if you start looking at a particular period you begin not at the top with ideas, you begin at the bottom; with the way people get their living, the economic and social dimension of history which in the past was simply regarded – until I suppose, even in the 1960s – very largely regarded as an optional extra by historians; you know, an extra chapter that Macaulay puts in, you see, when he's not thinking about the really important bits. Well now we know that it is not an optional extra; it is absolutely central, though it's not the only thing.

Inherent in, at least the popular understanding of Marx and Marxism, is the notion of progress and one way that one might read the history which you have written is as a dialogue between a nineteenth-century idea of progress, in which progress has an almost moral weight in the societies of the West obviously, with a twentieth century that begins to learn to question the morality that is associated with progress. Is that a fair way of trying to read part, certainly, of your history?

What you have in the nineteenth century is a belief that progress is both material and moral. In the twentieth century the case for material progress is far more convincing even than it was in the 19th century; no question about it at all, but if that was the only way of defining progress we would have to define the twentieth century, in spite of its appalling sacrifices, as a period of progress. At the same time there has now been a break between the belief that material progress automatically also leads to moral progress, to better education, to better behaviour, public behaviour, private behaviour, to an advance, if you like, of the values of civility; because these, from 1914 on, have been if anything in regression. Perhaps they will revive once again, but reading a certain number of the postmodern ideologists one is sceptical.

You argue that at the end of this century, where we are now, there is a major shift, the image that you choose is of tectonic plates in which there is a shift, as it were, in the crust below the surface of the earth. Does that suggest that there were continuities that run certainly from the nineteenth century through 1914, where your history begins, to 1917 up to now, or are we to see history in this century as this series of tectonic plates, rubbing together, shifting?

My argument in the book is that there are continuities which run, if you like, from the new Stone Age until the 1950s or the 1960s: that, to some extent, everything that happened, including the earlier phases of bourgeois liberal capitalism, used, assimilated, adapted this inheritance. Family structure is a very good example of this; it is not something created, it had existed before and it was used. My argument is that in the third quarter of the nineteenth century the rate, the impetus, the weight, if you like, of dramatic historical change is so great and so sudden and so rapid that these things are disintegrating.

And to that extent we are indeed facing an unknown and unprecedented situation.

At the beginning of Age of Extremes *you suggest that we live in an ahistorical age, an age where, particularly, the young, perhaps, have no sense, as their parents and their grandparents would have done, of their own histories and the histories of the groups to which they belong. What is the evidence that suggests itself to you to support that idea, that there is a loss of the historical sense at the moment?*

For anyone that teaches history in the United States the evidence is fairly obvious that people simply do not know the most elementary things about it. I quote somewhere the fact that a very intelligent student comes around to ask his professor, 'You talk about the Second World War. Does that mean there was a first one?' And yet that is not a joke; it's a serious question.

And yet those very same students, American students, are probably no longer defining themselves as American, but are thinking of themselves as African American or Italian American or German Americans or Native Americans; in other words, they are consciously attempting to retrieve some kind of history about themselves that their parents and their grandparents, in particular if they had come from Europe, tried to conceal?

That's right; one more reason why historians are essential is because what they are trying to recover is an invented and mythological and fantastic history, which in some instances isn't even history at all. I mean it's pure invention. It is our business and I spend a good deal of my time trying to demonstrate that mythology is not history.

And nor is 'heritage' history?

A lot of heritage is also mythological, or at least mythified.

The last section of your book is something particularly rare in historians; an attempt to look forward, not with any kind of exact sense of prediction, but at least to take stock of what the issues confronting us are; to do with population, the environment and ecological concerns and so forth, but you end, if I may quote, 'The price of failure, that is to say, the alternative to a changed society, is darkness.' What is that darkness?

The darkness is living, getting used to living, in ways which are inhuman. I've tried to say this before in different connections, and I'll try to say it again; when we predict catastrophe most people think that what we are predicting is something like a volcanic eruption or an earthquake, but in actual fact we have been living through, we are living through, slow motion catastrophes, so that people get used to normality in situations which should not be regarded as normal. I first got this impression vividly when I saw, years ago, in Northern Ireland the bombs being dropped, the war being conducted, in environments which were the exact opposite; ordinary housing estates, outside Woolworths, and I saw we are getting used to this. We are getting used to this and we shouldn't and I am warning against a world in which we get used to living under conditions which our fathers and grandfathers correctly have regarded as intolerable.

RAYMOND WILLIAMS: CULTURE AND HISTORY

Steve Woodhams

PROBABLY THE MAJORITY OF epitaphs for Raymond Williams have emphasised that he was a leading socialist intellectual. More suitable though is one found in *Raymond Williams: Making Connections* stating simply that Raymond Williams was 'one of the towering intellectuals of the postwar period'.[1] What is wrong, indeed ironically wrong, with the qualification is its tendency to ghettoise Williams in a special camp reserved for socialist intellectuals only. An apparent awareness of that trap is the first, though by no means the only asset which makes *Making Connections* a welcome book.

There is a second reason for opening on this point. In their introduction the Eldridges cite Michael Rustin's comment that as an active socialist Williams remains almost entirely ignored by the mainstream labour movement.[2] There has, in other words, been a continued contradiction in Williams' political efforts. Enormously influential for three or more generations of what might be termed an independent or non-aligned left, Williams largely failed to gain a hearing from what remains an intellectually shallow labour movement. The failure, to date, of a reply equal to the scope of Williams work from either liberal or conservative intellectual traditions, contrasted with the hearing that figures from these perspectives have gained in mainstream politics, only makes the situation all the more alarming. These comments refer though only to the situation in England. That in Wales has been markedly different – a contrast that must be kept to the fore if we are to fully appreciate the life of Raymond Williams.

In commencing a review article with these general political statements we come immediately to what increasingly became the heart of Williams thinking. Born in the border country close by the Black Mountains, Williams followed the well-worn path eastwards into England. While the great majority of those who had gone that way before had done so as paid labour, Williams was not the first to go into England in order to continue an education begun in Wales. At Cambridge he joined the Communist Party, working as a member of the Writers' Group. One product of that activity was a booklet written with Eric Hobsbawm favouring the Russians in the then current

Soviet-Finnish dispute. Called up in 1940, he saw action in Normandy as a tank commander, before being demobbed and returning to Cambridge to complete his studies.

The later 1940s were personally, as well a politically, hurtful for Williams. Looking back he has since commented on an isolation that he had to write his way out of.[3] The early results of this effort were a range of books which probably established Williams as a writer. Two of these, *Reading and Criticism* (1950) and *Preface to Film* (1954) arose directly out of his adult education classes. The others, *Drama from Ibsen to Eliot* (1952) and *Drama in Performance* (1954), were to be significant for Williams' academic future. A few years later these works were to be augmented by three books which brought Williams to the attention of a wider public; *Culture and Society* (1958), *Border Country* (1960) and *The Long Revolution* (1961). One outcome from this already rapidly growing body of work was that in 1961 he left adult education teaching to take up an appointment to a lectureship at Cambridge. The volume of work in the subsequent years was by any standards remarkable.

❏ Textbook Williams

Yet it is the scope of the work that is perhaps the more startling and which makes any attempt at producing a full assessment of Williams a daunting task. Published in 1994, *Raymond Williams: Making Connections* is the product of a partnership whose places of work at least are ironically situated in the two subordinate states of mainland Britain. For John Eldridge this, it is true, means Scotland, but Lizzie Eldridge is in Wales, at the University of Glamorgan, with which Raymond Williams had had his own connections. An understanding of Wales in Williams though is not a main theme in *Making Connections*. Recognisable in the chapter on the 'trilogy', it remains marginal in discussion of Williams' politics.

In *Making Connections*, the Eldridges tackle the difficulty presented by the diversity of Williams' writing by making the work something of a textbook. The book compises ten chapters, five of these given over to either major non-fiction works: *Culture and Society*, *The Long Revolution*, *The Country and the City*, or to substantial areas of Williams' writing: 'media culture', 'drama and literature'. Two are devoted to what, for the present writer, was some of the most important of Williams' work, the novels: *Border Country*, *Second Generation* and *Fight*

RAYMOND WILLIAMS: CULTURE AND HISTORY

for Manod, (the 'trilogy'), *The Volunteers* and *Loyalties.* Three further chapters provide the reader with summaries and responses to selected other writings on Williams, and a short treatment of Williams' politics. In this connection it is interesting to note that the publisher includes the book under the heading of 'political sociology'. One attractive feature of *Making Connections* is that unlike so much contemporary cultural theory, it is written in an open and lucid manner, an achievement which is all the greater when we remember the dense style of Williams' own prose.

For reasons that are not entirely clear, the discussion of existing writings in chapter two is rather selective and confined to works by single authors only. Consequently a number of other writings go unexamined, or even unmentioned. Among the first group are Terry Eagleton (ed.) *Raymond Williams: Critical Perspectives* (1989),[4] and Dowkin and Roman (eds) *Views Beyond the Border Country* (1993). Another work by single author not cited by the Eldridges is Nicolas Tredell's *Uncancelled Challenge: The Work of Raymond Williams* (1990). Other edited collections include Morgan and Preston *Raymond Williams: Politics, Education, Letters* (1993), and an issue of *News From Nowhere* (no. 6, 1989), 'Raymond Williams: Third Generation'. The citing of these texts here is intended to make possible a fuller appreciation of Williams. Not referenced here though are a number of articles on Williams, and the writer would be pleased to learn of other publications not listed by the Eldridges or myself. For a comprehensive list of Williams' own work and those about him by others, the impressive bibliography completed by Alan O'Connor which can be found in the aforementioned book edited by Eagleton and in O'Connor's own *Raymond Williams: Writing, Culture, Politics* (1989), is much recommended.

❏ **Against elitism**

Culture and Society was not, as we have already noted, the first of Williams' books but it is probably remembered by many as his first work of major influence. The Eldridges follow the book's structure commenting on each part in turn. *Culture and Society* begins with one of the major themes throughout the whole of Williams work, the tracing forward of certain 'keywords'. 'Williams' method', the Eldridges note, 'is to study the language of individual thinkers rather than to deal with a number of abstract problems'.[5] This was not to remain

Williams' only, or even primary, method in the future, though the attendance to actual use of language was always an important empirical referent. *Making Connections* traces through Williams' chosen speakers, noting along the way that 'For Williams, it is [Matthew] Arnold's definition of culture in *Culture and Anarchy* (1869) that gives the tradition a single watchword.'[6] The tradition, of course, is that mirrored in the title of Williams' work. The Eldridges' treatment is sympathetic, broadly agreeing with the aim of *Culture and Society*, to wrestle the term culture away from its elite moorings, reinforced by institutions such as Cambridge, and extend its reference to a way of life which includes the institutions of the labour movement and the cooperative solidarity that has characterised working-class life in many parts.

Williams' effort is reinforced by the Eldridges who take forward the criticisms of Arnold to a later essay 'A hundred years of culture and anarchy'.[7] The essay comments on the Reform League and a demonstration in Hyde Park. Where Arnold had referred to the threat to 'culture' represented by this largely working-class gathering, Williams' argument is that through their varied institutions and patterns of life, working-class people had always sought to extend education and learning to enrich still further the lives of the majority.

Culture and Society was an attempt to stop an elite tradition, for which culture was a limited resource which, if spread too thin, would lose its quality. The argument is taken a stage further in *The Long Revolution* which sets out to offer an alternative theory, supported by a number of empirical histories. In textbook style, *Making Connections* provides a useful summary of the more obviously theoretical first part of *The Long Revolution*. Tabling three definitions of 'culture', the Eldridges place alongside these the type of analysis necessary for their investigation.[8] The device of a table is used elsewhere in *Making Connections*. In the preceding chapter the different understandings of the term culture are set down against particular historical periods.[9] The practice of setting out what can otherwise seem a historical and conceptual maze in such a manner is a useful one, enabling a reader not familiar with cultural theory and history to more quickly grasp some start points. The density of Williams' prose can be far from helpful here, and students would be well advised to use *Making Connections*, or similar text, before reading Williams in the original. The different case studies of the second part of *The Long Revolution* are summarised neatly, though the long essay on Britain as it entered the 1960s, is left aside. The decision, whether by the publishers or by Williams, to reprint this essay 25 years later as part one of *Toward 2000* is noted by the Eldridges, and has always struck the present writer as not perhaps the best choice, given the forward looking stance of the later book.

As already suggested, for the present writer it is the fictional work which is amongst the most important of all Williams' output. Two chapters of *Making Connections* are given to the novels, the first to the 'trilogy' and the second to *The Volunteers* and *Loyalties* . For reasons that are not made clear, the last of Williams' fiction writings, the two-volume *People of the Black Mountains* is ignored. In *Making Connections* the trilogy is linked through the themes of past–present–future. Under this general pattern are set down a number of other connections, including that of 'between generations'. One source on which the Eldridges base their commentary of the trilogy is a series of lectures, published in *Writing and Society* (1983) as 'The Tenses of Imagination'.

❑ **Autobiographical dimension**

The autobiographical dimension of the first volume, *Border Country*, in particular has been commented on before.[10] Perhaps what needs to be kept in mind is that at the time of writing his first published novel, Williams felt more distanced from Wales than at any other time. Certainly at no point is there any romanticising of Wales, nor is there creation of a mythical homeland from which a certainty of identity may simply be put on. Instead the relationship between Wales and England is so arranged as to make it impossible for either to be made a security against the intrusions of the other. The tension is illustrated through another of the connections listed by the Eldridges, that 'between memories and current experience/feelings'.[11] We can find some of these elements grouped together in the following passage: '... the awareness and experience of the continued tension between past, present and future often leads Williams' characters towards a new way of seeing and/or feeling, resulting in the familiar appearing strange or the strange becoming familiar'.[12] There is an example of this near the beginning of the third volume, *The Fight for Manod*. Before finally accepting the offer of the contract to study views on Manod, Mathew Price goes to meet Robert Lane, the civil servant charged with examining the feasibility of the project. On the wall is a map, not of Manod the place, but of Manod the plan. Looking away through the windows of Lane's office, Mathew is struck by the apparent strangeness of the city in which he lives, as its contours become marked out by the lines of electric lights sending out their beams to head off the encroaching darkness. The view of the familiar become strange, which Mathew sees out of the window, is set off against unfamiliar lines of a map on a wall against which stood the name Manod, from the actual land that was that place as Mathew recalled it in is memory.[13]

❏ Continuity of generations

Yet it is the connections between generations that makes for the full continuity of story across the three works and which allows the reader to engage in so many of the tensions and possibilities that go to make up the layers of the various characters. In *Border Country* the generations are typified in the characters of father and son. It is not possible for the same work in the same place to be carried on and physical movement becomes a necessity. With this movement comes a change of where a living might be made, and the means through which it might be achieved. Yet in certain fundamental ways the patterns of life; forming relationships, setting down a place to live, bringing on a new generation, still have to be carried forward. As in so much of Williams there exists that tension between the deep flows of life, the continuity, and the changing forms through which those flows must be realised.

We can better see these themes if we look at two or three characters from the novels a little further. In *Second Generation* we are presented with perhaps the strongest of Williams' female characters. For me Kate Owen is a far more significant character than the *New Left Review* interviewers seem to have thought.[14] In *Making Connections* Kate is discussed in terms of the potential for sexual freedom with which she experiments. Yet this in a sense is only part of something larger. The Eldridges identify this in a critical passage. Kate is one of ' ... the huddling survivors of a generation that has seen every chance of a new life deferred, and had acquiesced in the deferment. This is what it meant to be born into a deferred generation, into war, into the slow collapse of hope.'[15]

Kate is the same generation as Williams. Where, in *Border Country*, Will had crossed the border from Welsh working class to Cambridge and become Mathew, Kate had been prevented by her gender as well as class. Yet beyond this, still further blocks had come in the way. The hoped for change that the war had given Williams and the fictional

Kate was to be deferred in the years immediately after. We can begin to understand this experience from what Williams has had to say about his own thoughts and feelings during this period. As far as the bigger political context was concerned Williams has commented that 'The rhetoric of victory in 1945 is in a sense fair enough, but it shouldn't convince anyone unless it is immediately qualified by the realities of 1947–48.'[16] Referring to himself but still focusing on the larger political scene, he comments: ' ... I was so thrown out of my early expectations, as a young man and a soldier in the war, by the events of 1947 that I went into a kind of retreat for a year or two, ...'[17]

In the same interview and elsewhere Williams fills out the political with the personal events and feelings of the period and at the same time presents his own feelings in terms closer to the characters in the novels. The years after the war were 'a kind of cancellation of the certainties I had assumed in childhood ... The crisis came to me on the death of my father.'[18] Referring to his own family, which at this time included two babies, Williams has commented that 'You could say I had to support them, but in real terms, after the various crises, it was much more that they supported me.'[19]

In the fiction, Kate is less able than Mathew in *Border Country* or again in *The Fight for Manod*, to come to an adjustment with her history. Kate belongs to the same generation as Mathew. Yet where he seems to find some means of reconciling the borders of Wales and England, of class, and of the village and university, when we rejoin Kate in *The Fight for Manod* she lives in London. She has achieved the place of the obligatory female on every Labour Party committee, yet beyond that there remain divisions both in herself and outside in the world, between which no means of connection and continuity have been found.

The theme of generation is continued in *The Volunteers* and in *Loyalties*. As the Eldridges remark, *The Volunteers* was written during the same period as *The Fight for Manod*, yet in style the two books are distinct. The former carries forward strands from *Border Country* and *Second Generation*, constantly linking up pieces from each, most obviously in the lead characters of Mathew Price and Peter Owen. Wales and Manod exist both as places and as ideas of what might have been and still could be if the opportunity is taken and used in the right way. *The Volunteers* is written in the more popular style of a political thriller. Set in the future (1988), Williams attempts to let play the living through of alternative social relations which in *The Fight for Manod* remain only as possibilities.

As the Eldridges point out, generation is again present as a theme in *The Volunteers*, though it must be said that its centrality is much more apparent in *Loyalties*. Rather misleadingly, *Loyalties* is cited as Williams' last completed fictional work, '*People of the Black Mountains* remaining an unfinished project'.[20] Yet of course there are two volumes published, though in *Making Connections* they are left unexamined. Had they been completed, the theme of generation would once again have been seen to assert itself strongly, though over a much longer time. As it is, where, in the trilogy, three generations require three volumes for their connections to work through, the structure of *Loyalties* allows all three to exist between a single set of covers.

The different generations are marked out by events, histories and places. The Black Mountains and Spain in the mid-1930s are displaced by Normandy in 1944. Where Cambridge augments each of these in the earlier parts of the novel, this is in turn displaced by London in the later sequences. Where Spain and Normandy serve as such poignant historical markers of one period, they are replaced in the lives of later generations by Vietnam. Yet the difference of experience means that the replacement cannot be of the same measure. ' ... it was both for our dad's generation ... The struggle in the pits and the struggle for Spain.'[21] The measure of this difference is set down coldly in the reply, 'They're not going to fight in Vietnam though, are they?'[22] The reference to fighting need not be taken only to refer to armed conflict between rival soldiers, but to the immediacy of economic and political struggle, the comparison with the pit.

❑ **Structures of feeling**

In *Making Connections* these tensions and differences are recognised in the contrasts of loyalties between classes. For Norman Braose his upper-middle-class background and his communist allegiance sets in train a loyalty which yet demands isolation, in the form of a 1930s Cambridge spy, for it to be lived out. In contrast, Nesta, who as a young women had an affair with Norman, and her eventual husband Bert, express their loyalty in and through the pressures forcing themselves and others together. An 'unquestioned adherence to a particular way of life'.[23]

Given that *Making Connections* is primarily a textbook covering major issues of Williams academic writing, inclusion of the novels is only to be welcomed. As the Eldridges note, it is in the novels that Williams can be seen to be thinking through many of his ideas. Here I have emphasised those of generation, memories and experience, borders and the structure of past, present and future. In addition to these the Eldridges note those of language and communication, community and that most difficult of terms, 'structure of feeling'. This last is discussed most expansively in the chapter on 'Drama and literature' and that on 'The trilogy'. According to the Eldridges, the term is first fully used by Williams in 'Preface to Film'. More recently in 'The Tenses of Imagination', from which the Eldridges draw in their discussion of the trilogy, Williams refers to a structure of feeling in terms of '... an active formation ... a connection with something fully knowable but not yet fully known'.[24] The Eldridges rightly recognise that the term is not meant as a concept in the usual academic sense.

In this sense it is not to the thought of Raymond Williams that we should refer, but to the thinking. It is the active process which is important. Stuart Hall perhaps expresses this point best when he distinguishes between a cerebral activity of thinking characteristic of much academic writing and a lived activity of thinking which he experienced with Raymond Williams.[25] In the same manner, a structure of feeling is an attempt to move beyond the authorised or recorded version, the selection of a past which in time becomes its history. It is rather the real, and as such, knowable community, and within this the patterns of living and communication, upon which the existence of the community is dependent.

Throughout *Making Connections* these same terms are rightly returned to again and again. Yet, even then, the danger of abstracting them from the life remains. Given that *Making Connections* is, as I say, primarily a textbook, inclusion of Williams' political life as the content of the last chapter is only to be welcomed. In general the points made there are fair. I would, however, suggest a danger if *Making Connections* and others of its style were to be the only books on Raymond Williams. The problem here of course is the requirements of the academic world. Students must prepare their essays and for this the necessity is to submit a piece of writing in an orthodox style. One part of this is the analysis of concepts: a book or article is distilled down until the precise words are sufficiently isolated for their inspection and to this end the fault is too few books on Williams in the style of the

Eldridge volume. My complaint though is that isolating the terms – experience, structure of feeling, community etc. – denies the possibility of understanding them as part of an ongoing and living argument. It is this abstracting of the ideas from the life, of freezing the words into concepts, stopping the actual thinking so as to leave finished thoughts, that is for me the problem.

❏ Another Williams

We can get a flavour of this tendency if we look at *Culture and Society*. Looking back nearly 40 years, *Culture and Society* appears to us now as a very solid work from an established figure. Yet it must be remembered that at the time of writing Williams was a young teacher in adult education who had graduated from Cambridge in 1946. *Culture and Society* came from the experience of adult education teaching on the one hand and, on the other, a keen awareness of the dominant tradition as it was handed down from Cambridge. In short, it was an intervention – intellectual, yes, but also, and unavoidably, political. In order to appreciate this the students must turn from the textbook to the history and, within that, the life. It is from this last perspective that I suggest another book can be written, an account of another Raymond Williams as it were.

The structure I suggest would be something like the following;

> Growing up into the 1930s
> The war experience [and army education]
> The project of *Politics and Letters*
> Adult Education
> Isolation and the Cold War
> Emergence into the 'new left'
> May Day Manifesto and the National Convention of the Left
> The Socialist Society
> The 1984–85 Miners Strike and Community
> Towards 2000

Here there is not space to set down the contents of each of these chapters separately. The emphasis though would be historical and political, locating Williams in terms of the struggles with which he identified and the sort of political formations within which he worked. Before the war the issues were the great international struggles, Abyssinia,

China, Spain; these in turn were reflected in the Left Book Club groups, and the peoples' front against the policies of the National Government. The war itself would need to be addressed in some detail, as too would the atmosphere of postwar Cambridge. *Politics and Letters*, adult education, and the events of 1956, would have running through them the question of how the Cold War in practice served to keep people apart. To this end Williams' own political position would need to be offset against those in the Communist Party and those on the Labour left. The Campaign for Nuclear Disarmament would be a focal point in discussion of the years 1956 through to 1962, after which the difficult question of the position Williams represented in relation to the Labour Party would have to be tackled. The National Convention of the Left remains an unwritten history, but sufficiently recent for oral accounts to be readily available. While the order of the book would be broadly chronological, there would be a need to look always sideways, to include other political formations and the relationship between these and Williams. Similarly there is a need to record how the events of the earlier years made for a framework of experience through which the more recent events could be understood. As with the treatment of Williams' fiction in *Making Connections*, the experience of generation would be a guiding thread. Indeed the question may have to be faced that the commitment to an intellectual socialism, characteristic of a number of Williams' peers, was the result of the experience of a particular generation and not therefore repeatable in same manner today, however much we may wish it otherwise.

A historical and political approach would not ignore Williams' theoretical contribution to so many areas of intellectual work. Rather these would be set against particular experiences and the struggles with which Williams identified. As such there would necessarily be an emphasis on the earlier years of his life, since it was during these that the most significant learning took place. As he has himself remarked more than once, his experience in the years 1945 to 1948 meant that Williams was ready to meet the setbacks which many on the left were to suffer in years to come. Two examples of this are, first the recognition of the nature of the Wilson Government in 1966 based on the experience of the Labour Party and Government in the years after the war. But perhaps the more immediate to Williams was the experience from the same period of the failure of *Politics and Letters*, and his determination in 1962 that whatever its shortcomings – and there were certainly a number in the coming years – *New Left Review* should be allowed to continue. Later, looking back to 1956 when so many intellectual socialists came out from the Communist Party and attempted to create a new political formation, Williams asks where they were in 1947.

In summing up the history I would wish to emphasise two points. First, that unless the full measure of the years 1945 to 1948 is taken into account, much of Williams' later political and intellectual life may not be fully understood. Second, that the position reached by many after 1956 was that which Williams was seeking to construct a decade earlier, but which the pressures of those years prevented others from recognising.

Finally, though, the most important value of a historical and political account would not be the past but the future, and to this end *Making Connections* can only be of benefit. For this venture the question becomes what use might we make of Williams as we pass through the year 2000 and enter the next century. To ask that might yet be to ask, what chance socialism?

Steve Woodhams teaches at the University of Luton and is a regular contributor to Socialist History.

NOTES

1. John and Lizzie Eldridge, *Raymond Williams: Making Connections*, (Routledge 1994).
2. Michael Rustin, 'Raymond Williams 1921–1988', *Radical Philosophy*, 1988.
3. Raymond Williams, *Politics and Letters: Interviews with New Left Review* (New Left Books, 1979), p. 77.
4. Terry Eagleton (ed.), *Raymond Williams: Critical Perspectives* (Polity Press, 1989).
5. Eldridge and Eldridge, *Making Connections*, p. 46.
6. Ibid., p. 51.
7. Raymond Williams, *Problems in Materialism and Culture* (Verso, 1980), pp. 3–11.
8. Eldridge and Eldridge, *Making Connections*, p. 78.
9. Ibid., p. 62.
10. Williams, *Politics and Letters*, p. 283.
11. Eldridge and Eldridge, *Making Connections*, p. 140.
12. Ibid., p. 141.
13. Raymond Williams, *The Fight for Manod* (Hogarth Press, 1988), p. 17.

14. Williams, *Politics and Letters*, pp. 287–295.
15. Raymond Williams, *Second Generation* (Hogarth Press, 1988), quoted in Eldridge and Eldridge, *Making Connections*, p. 151.
16. Eagleton, *Raymond Williams*, p. 177.
17. Ibid.
18. Ibid., p. 183.
19. Williams, *Politics and Letters*, p. 64.
20. Eldridge and Eldridge, *Making Connections*, p. 166.
21. Raymond Williams, *Loyalties* (Hogarth Press, 1989), quoted in Eldridge and Eldridge, *Making Connections*, p. 171.
22. Williams, *Loyalties*, p. 220.
23. Eldridge and Eldridge, *Making Connections*, p. 170.
24. Raymond Williams, *Writing in Society* (Verso, 1983).
25. The distinction was made by Stuart Hall in a televised discussion of the life and work of Raymond Williams: 'Raymond Williams – A Tribute', Large Door Productions, 28 February 1988, Channel Four.

REVIEWS

HISTORY MANICURED?

Raphael Samuel, *Theatres of Memory*, Vol. I: *Past and Present in Contemporary Culture* (Verso, London, 1994), xiv & 479pp., ISBN 0 86091 2094, £19.95.

Raphael Samuel has written a complex, challenging, sometimes puzzling book; a large compendium, the first of three planned volumes, it has numerous ramifications. Its fundamental business is with how history writing is now being 'reconceptualised' (is so odious a word really necessary?) in the light of new conditions and techniques. It is breaking away from the conventional academic mould: no bad thing, in the author's view, since this has grown remote from the common man's interests and 'encourages inbreeding, introspection, sectarianism' (p. 3). The setting for this breakaway has been a vertiginous series of changes in taste, fashion and direction in other spheres of British life since the war. Architecture has moved from functional to decorative, from modernising to preserving, from stone to brick, from masculine to feminine. There has been a growing appetite for the antique, or pseudoantique; imitation old watches for instance have been part of the 'nostalgia industry' (p. 91), known by another horrid title, borrowed from the French, *Retrochic*.

Samuel's familiarity with the minutiae of these portentous shifts must strike a reader as phenomenal, particularly an unobservant reader who has lived through them without realising that they were taking place. Here we have an explorer who has, so to speak, sniffed at every lamp post, and can catalogue every whiff and puff. It is a revelation, even if a nagging doubt may persist about how much of this brave new world was concocted by salesmen and advertisers, pulling the wool of a new heaven and a new earth over our eyes. Our expert himself does not always seem sure. Much, he admits, has been merely 'playful and theatrical' (p. 95). Was there really a 'cultural revolution' in the 1960s, some of it fuelled by Pop art? – a Pop which, he recognises, 'follows well-worn poetical tropes', and amounts to little but 'a kind of adolescent, or pre-pubescent keening' (p. 90). It is less unrealistic to speak of 'the sexual revolution of the 1970s' (p. 114); it needs to be added that this has been tolerated, if not exactly foisted on the country, by way of a harmless substitute for real social-political change.

Of the urgent need for such change, the lost opportunity after 1945, and the impasse it has got Britain to, the book has little to say. It is concerned less with a better future than with modes of feeling about the past and people, and wanting to preserve it. They extend to conservation of the countryside, of whose urgent importance there can be no doubt; there can be grave doubt, though, as to how much success can be achieved without the nationalisation of the land which ought to have been carried out by the nineteenth-century bourgeoisie. Samuel does not raise this question; yet even access to the countryside, which he rightly thinks of as a most valuable gain, is today being blocked off once more. How many country houses, or stately homes, deserve to be kept, is not so clear. There has been strong criticism, notably by Patrick Wright, of the ideology of 'Heritage', according to which everything on British soil is to be cherished as a national inheritance, whoever actually owns it and whoever it can be sold to. Samuel rejects, surely too summarily, the argument that much of this has been a Tory confidence-trick (p. 24 ff.). He welcomes the more populist slant that has been latterly given to Heritage. Not the country house, he maintains, but the cottage, has become its central feature, the humble abode of most of our ancestors. Unquestionably we ought to be interested in it. But we ought not to be lulled by folk museums, as Samuel confesses it is sometimes easy to be (p. 281), into forgetting that the old village was dominated by squire and parson living at its inhabitants' expense, the lord in a fine mansion while the farm labourer was left in what was often an insanitary hovel.

❏ **New methods**

We shall never be rid of such class division and exploitation if we allow ourselves to forget these things. This is the lesson that postwar Marxist historians set themselves to carry to the Labour movement. They forgot, as the Scottish nationalist poets were forgetting in another way, that they were trying to catch the attention of men and women with no habit of reading and little general knowledge for new ideas to nest in. Samuel is an enthusiast for the up-to-date methods which have been devised for initiating ordinary folk, and above all schoolchildren, into the shadowy past: open-air museums, guided tours, 'Heritage trails', 'living history' with participants in period costumes, *son et lumière*. He is convinced that, educationally at least, all this has been brilliantly effective. And yet the generation which has grown up with it is, to an unprecedented degree, a problem generation.

These methods are simple, direct, exciting: they make the past something tangible. They can be an excellent curtain-raiser, but, like serious historical writing, for contrary reasons are inadequate by themselves. By itself, a 'cult of the cottage' risks infection from something similar to the Victorian sentimentality about the village home where '

> The roses round the door
> Make me love Mother more'.

Heritage talk *may,* Samuel admits, savour of 'an attempt to escape from class' (p. 246). Not, that is, by abolishing class inequality, but by pretending that it no longer exists, if indeed it ever did. Tory spokesmen since the war have harped a great deal on this reposeful thought. Samuel, as a good socialist, cannot altogether reconcile himself to his own thesis. Our new vista of the past, he declares, is 'inconceivably more democratic' than any earlier ones (p. 160). Yet, sad to say, it is Toryism that has profited, not the left (p. 162). It cannot be accidental, he remarks truly, that all this concern for history dates from the same decade as the long-term 'withdrawal of the working class from politics' (p. 190). History offered up like this 'invites us to play games with the past and to pretend that we are at home in it' (p. 196). It may be as well to recall that the country which has developed 'living history' most elaborately is America, where it can still be perilous to be suspected of being a liberal, to say nothing of a socialist.

Samuel conducts us into a variety of intriguing purlieus. He has much to say about Dickens, and shows he is no mean literary critic, though he is discussing the novelist mainly as seen through the prism of cinema and television. An 'Afterword' provides a sketch of the whole field of today's historical thinking, theorising and research, with their fallibilities and sometimes falsifications. Essentially, it is clear, Samuel stands firmly by the principle that historians should *not* retreat from 'moral and political argument' (p. 244). Everyone who has been touched by the magic wand of history – most of all those who teach it – ought to read and enjoy this well-written, well-illustrated book, and argue fiercely about it.

V.G. Kiernan

Victor Kiernan is Emeritus Professor of History at the University of Edinburgh.

MARGOT HEINEMANN REMEMBERED

David Margolies and Maroula Joannou, eds, *Heart of the Heartless World: Essays in Cultural Resistance in Memory of Margot Heinemann* (Pluto Press, London, 1995), xiii & 223pp., ISBN 0 7453 0982 8, £14.95, paperback.

This volume of essays by friends and colleagues of Margot Heinemann was conceived as a *Festschrift* when the respected scholar and Marxist was still alive. It now appears as a memorial to a remarkable personality whose death in 1992 robbed the left of one of its most committed and inspiring activists. For over 50 years, in a multi-faceted life, Heinemann championed the socialist cause, as a communist, as a trade union researcher, as a writer and finally as a Cambridge-based literary critic. She worked closely with the Historians' Group, collaborating with Noreen Branson on *Britain in the 1930s* and co-editing a collection of A.L. Morton's essays as late as 1990. All the contributors to this book were inspired by contact with her at varying stages in her long career; but despite this it is an uneven and eclectic collection. Veteran Marxist historians Victor Kiernan and Christopher Hill do not disappoint with their thoughtful essays on seventeenth-century literature, a subject which so concerned Heinemann herself; while Eric Hobsbawm's funeral address pays affectionate tribute to a close comrade of 55 years standing. Her former party cultural committee colleague Colin Chambers writes on Unity Theatre but adds little to his earlier book-length history of the company. Heinemann's younger mainly academic associates concentrate on detailed analysis of individual texts and contribute what to the present reviewer are largely arcane criticisms of interest only to those familiar with current postmodernist concerns. This literary bias gives a certain imbalance to the book and as such the volume ultimately does not do full justice to Heinemann; she was after all not only the author of *Puritanism and Theatre* but also of polemical Communist Party pamphlets like *The Tories and How to Beat Them* and studies for Labour Research like *Britain's Coal* and *The Wages Front*. More space could have been devoted to her political activities. The most rewarding piece deals specifically with Heinemann's writings, and that is Andy Croft on her only fictional work, *The Adventurers* published in 1960 at the fag-end of Socialist Realism. He carefully establishes the historical context and actually makes one want to go and read this neglected novel. Croft also whets the appetite for a full-length study or biography of Heinemann; perhaps someone should undertake this soon while many who knew her are still around.

David Morgan

David Morgan *is a member of the* Socialist History *editorial team.*

MORRIS MISREPRESENTED

Fiona MacCarthy, *William Morris: A Life for Our Time*, (Faber and Faber, London, 1994), 780pp., ISBN 0 571 14250 8, £25 hardback.

It is with some trepidation that any admirer of Morris aware of MacCarthy's previous work on Eric Gill picks up this biography; for that Gill book was full of lurid details of the sculptor's sex life, from incest to paedophilia. Fortunately MacCarthy can find nothing like this to compromise Morris's reputation. Instead she can merely indulge in some bizarre, but harmless, Freudian psychosexual interpretations of his literary works; she improbably detects foot fetishism in one poem (p. 205). She is able to dwell at length on the two affairs of Jane Morris with Rossetti and W.S. Blunt, but in Morris' correspondence with Georgiana Burne-Jones she finds nothing more sensational than friendly confidences.

This biography's selling point, and the focus of the book launch publicity, is its apparent new discovery of Morris' revolutionary socialism; at least newspaper articles and radio interviews with the author gave that impression. That MacCarthy is far from being the first in the field with this discovery might well pass by the general reader whom she is mainly addressing, but it may be considered akin to plagiarism by others, like many readers of this journal, with more than a cursory interest in Morris. Those aware of the long history of research into Morris's politics, from Robin Page Arnot in 1934 (whom MacCarthy only cites in the bibliography) to E.P. Thompson in 1955 (whom she can't so easily ignore), will not be entirely satisfied with MacCarthy's approach; despite the volume's length of over 750 pages it adds little that is new to appreciating his stature as a figure of the left, and as we near the centenary year of his death in 1996 we must hope there are others to reassess his significance as a socialist thinker 'for our time'.

Admittedly, this biography's aim is primarily popularisation and its limitations are partly dictated by literary convention; but by following a soap-opera script of personalities and romantic relationships, MacCarthy encounters difficulties tackling ideas and concepts. This is not to suggest it is without some redeeming features, such as the synthesis of recent scholarship; MacCarthy's handling of this rich and various material is on the whole ably done. Jan Marsh on the Morris women, Jane and May; Harvey and Press on Morris as entrepreneur; Nicholas Salmon on his political journalism; Norman Kelvin's scrupulous edition of the collected letters; such researches enable MacCarthy to put all aspects of his multi-faceted life into perspective, and extensive coverage is given to his political activities, an admirable achievement for a popular biography.

It is at the tone that one baulks; it tends to the brash phrase of lazy tabloid journalism and thus trivialises its subject; an attitude that is more disappointing since the author is current president of the William Morris Society. Faced with the streetcorner speaking Morris, MacCarthy is like a curious explorer lighting on some newly discovered rare and exotic species. She writes incredulously: 'What are we to make of Morris driving himself onwards from one nerve-racking meeting to another through the icy winter months of 1887?' (p. 557). To the socialist, Morris' rage at injustice and his selfless dedication to 'the cause' remain continually inspiring; to MacCarthy he becomes an object of curiosity or pity. His political campaigning is contrasted unfavourably with the charity work of his sister, the Anglican deaconess Isabella Gilmore, whom, she goes so far as to claim, understood the workers better than her brother (p. 559).

❏ Travesty

Rival biographers, including E.P. Thompson, are accused of overstressing his affinity with Marxism while neglecting his alleged anarchist sympathies. However, MacCarthy overstates her own case on this, judging his friendships with Kropotkin and Stepniak as evidence of fully-fledged adherence to anarchism as a creed. Even *News From Nowhere* is said to have 'a subversive, autobiographical sub-text for the Anarchists' (p. 585). Her own attachment to anarchism flows from her travesty of socialism as state control and Marxism as what went on in Stalin's USSR. The great failing of this book is its inadequate grasp of Morris' central role in developing a vernacular socialist language for Britain; which was achieved decades before Sidney

Webb devised Clause Four, with classic statements of principle like 'Socialism: Its Growth and Outcome'. It is not that she does not mention these facts, but that she judges this aspect antiquated and opts for a more 'user friendly' Morris as proto-green and near feminist; from this angle *A Dream of John Ball* is 'still modern' as 'a startling early exercise in sexual politics' (p. 548).

The book's ambitious subtitle appears an unnecessary constraint which at every turn she feels obliged to justify by finding contemporary resonances; many seem forced, unconvincing or just plain pretentious and should not have survived the editing process: as when Morris' stay at the German spa town of Bad Ems is compared to 'Resnais's film Last Year at Marienbad' (p. 234). The early poem 'The Life and Death of Jason' is ludicrously described as 'a Victorian version of pornography' (p. 206); returning from Iceland Morris is said to be suffering from 'a Victorian equivalent of jet-lag' (p. 309); most absurd of all an interview with *Pall Mall Gazette* is called a 'Victorian equivalent of Desert Island Discs' (p. 562). She is so addicted to these absurdly artificial contemporary parallels that they become a substitute for explanation of Morris' continuing relevance. These are the surface observations of the journalist-cum-professional biographer rather than the solidly based conclusions of the disciplined historian; it is the arrogance of the present redefining the past to suit its purpose.

Anyone searching for an easy-to-read, not too intellectually demanding study of Morris, will be eminently satisfied with this new lavishly illustrated life; but it nowhere supersedes Thompson and for an introduction into just how relevant Morris is 'for our time' it is best to look at either Asa Briggs' or Morton's selections of his writings.

David Morgan

REVOLUTIONARY LIVES

Kevin Morgan, *Harry Pollitt* (Manchester University Press, Manchester, 1993), 210pp., ISBN 0 7190 3243, £40 hardback

John Callaghan, *Rajani Palme Dutt: A Study in British Stalinism* (Lawrence and Wishart, London, 1993), 302pp., ISBN 0 85315 779 0, £16.99

The appearance of these two biographies is to be welcomed. Both of them are well researched and highly readable.

Harry Pollitt was born in Lancashire in 1890. His mother was a weaver and, at the age of twelve, he joined her to work half-time at a local textile mill; three years later he started his apprenticeship as a boilermaker, after which he was admitted to the Boilermakers' Society. Early on, the poverty and deprivation which he saw around him had a powerful influence on him and at the age of sixteen he joined the Independent Labour Party and then the British Socialist Party. He spoke frequently at open-air meetings throughout Lancashire and Yorkshire; a gifted orator, he attracted huge crowds. His bitter hatred of the capitalist system and his determination to end it remained with him for the rest of his life.

After the First World War started in 1914 he was engaged in antiwar activities. In 1918 he moved to East London and became a leading figure in the River Thames Shop Stewards' Movement. He was inspired by the 1917 Russian Revolution which had toppled the hated capitalist class and had, as he thought, 'put power into the hands of lads like me'. When Russia was invaded by Western powers, he was prominent in the 'Hands Off Russia' campaign.

In 1920 he became a member of the Communist Party while it was still in process of formation as the 'British Section' of the Communist International, which consisted of communist parties all over the world. In October 1925, in the run-up to the General Strike, he was one of the twelve communists arrested and charged with 'seditious libel and incitement to mutiny' and was sentenced to twelve months in prison.

In 1929 following the adoption of a much more sectarian policy by the Comintern, Pollitt became the party's General Secretary. He continued to regard industrial struggle as the priority; however, in 1933 came a fundamental change in policy. That year Hitler came to power in Germany and the huge German Communist Party (KPD) was suppressed together with the Social Democrats, while the trade unions were made illegal, so it was that the need for united action against fascism became paramount, and the former sectarian policies began to be discarded. From the beginning Pollitt was closely involved in anti-fascist movements: against the British Union of Fascists led by Mosley; in support of the fight against Franco in Spain – indeed he helped recruit volunteers for the British Battalion of the International Brigade and himself visited Spain on several occasions to make contact with them.

When, in 1939, Hitler invaded Poland and the Chamberlain government declared war on Germany, Pollitt called for a 'war on two fronts': in other words the defeat of Hitler but the removal of Chamberlain. However a message then arrived from the Comintern asserting that it was an 'imperialist war' which should be opposed. Pollitt stuck to his views but, at a Central Committee meeting, was defeated and obliged to step down as General Secretary. After the invasion of Russia in June 1941 he was reinstated, and from then on concentrated on mobilising people for victory over the fascist powers, addressing endless meetings, campaigning for a second front in Europe and for the elimination of bottlenecks in war factories, he also initiated the formation of various committees to draw up discussion documents on the way forward after the war.

Following the 1945 election, Pollitt advocated support for the Labour government but this approach changed with the onset of the Cold War. In 1950 many meetings were held to celebrate his 60th birthday. However, in 1956, after the Khrushchev revelations of Stalin's atrocities, he stood down as party secretary, although he remained its chairman until his death in 1960.

Morgan presents a sympathetic picture of Pollitt as a person, showing why he was so much liked and admired. What motivated him was not self-advancement – had that been the case, he would certainly have achieved high position as a union leader, or indeed as a Labour MP. But it was the desire to see the end of capitalist rule that dominated his life and this Morgan makes very clear. He draws upon sources hitherto unavailable – including personal correspondence between Pollitt, Dutt and Salme Dutt – which provides new insight into the arguments around policies and tactics.

Those who are familiar with the political background of the period will find much in the material which Morgan makes use of very enlightening. However, there is a problem for those who are not aware of events of the time. This is particularly the case with the postwar Attlee government. Morgan describes the acceptance by Pollitt in 1947 of the new policy put forward by the Communist Information Bureau (Cominform) but does not mention the event which triggered it off, the declaration by the US President Truman that 'communism' must be treated as the 'enemy' and the launch of anti-communist witch-hunts.

Morgan is somewhat disdainful about the Communist Party's programme *The British Road to Socialism,* issued in 1950, suggesting that it made no mention of the guaranteed right to 'contested elections'. In fact it advocated proportional representation in place of the undemocratic 'first past the post' system, something which the party had been arguing for since 1944. Morgan also speaks of the 'partial retreat' of the party into its own private world in 1950. But that was the year when it was largely responsible for collecting over a million signatures to a petition for the banning of nuclear weapons; it had also played a leading part in the dockers' dispute which in 1951 forced the Attlee government to repeal its anti-strike regulations.

Despite such reservations I found this book extremely interesting.

❏ **A different personality**

A very different kind of person was Rajani Palme Dutt whose life and work are the subject of Callaghan's book. Born in Cambridge in 1896, Dutt's father was an Indian doctor, his mother was a Swedish writer. They had many Indian visitors and, early on, Dutt became convinced of the need to free India from British rule. A boy of outstanding ability, he won a scholarship to Oxford University and, soon after arriving there in 1914, he joined the Independent Labour Party. The First World War had just begun, and from the start Dutt was engaged in anti-war activities. In 1916 he was imprisoned for six months as a conscientious objector; in 1917, after addressing a public meeting in support of the Bolsheviks in Russia, he was expelled from the University and only allowed back to take his final exams on condition that he would not participate in any public meeting while there.

Like Pollitt, Dutt was involved in the formation of the Communist Party in Britain and when, in 1921, on Lenin's recommendation, the *Labour Monthly* was launched as a journal aimed at the broad left, he became its editor and was to remain so for the next 50 years. His regular 'Notes of the Month' provided a highly readable analysis of the political scene; they were widely read by left-wing activists who were much influenced by them. These 'Notes' were accompanied by articles from many progressive writers.

While engaged in the formation of the British CP Dutt became acquainted with Salme Murrik, an Estonian revolutionary who had been sent to Britain by Lenin as a Comintern representative. She and Dutt were married in Stockholm in 1924, and Dutt's links with the Comintern were from then on firmly established. They went to live in Brussels for the next twelve years where, despite bouts of ill-health, Dutt was engaged in work for the Comintern's 'West European Bureau' and acted as British representative on its Colonial Bureau based in Paris. Throughout he kept closely in touch with the British party; as well as compiling his 'Notes of the Month' and overseeing the work of other writers in the *Labour Monthly* he produced several books. And when, after the 1926 General Strike, the Comintern developed a much more sectarian policy, Dutt was one of its chief supporters. However, with the rise of fascism, he was forced to change his attitude; He participated in the Comintern's seventh World Congress in 1935 and soon afterwards returned to Britain.

After the war broke out, Dutt took the lead in lending support to the Comintern line that it was an 'imperialist war' which should be opposed, and temporarily replaced Pollitt as the party's General Secretary. But after the Nazi attack on the Soviet Union he handed back the responsibility to Pollitt, although he was to remain a member of its Executive Committee for many years.

Despite the demise of the Comintern in 1943, support for the Soviet Union continued to be Dutt's priority. He always believed that the future of socialism throughout the world depended on its survival. And when, in 1956, the truth about Stalin's atrocities was revealed by Khrushchev, he caused much anger among party members by his attempts to brush aside these revelations. Again, in 1968, when the party expressed opposition to the Soviet intervention in Czechoslovakia, Dutt disagreed and tried, unsuccessfully, to get the decision overturned. He died in 1974.

❏ **Positive aspects**

One of the most positive aspects of Dutt's life was his devotion to the anti-colonial struggle – indeed it seems likely that Lenin's insistence on the right of all nations to self-determination was one of the factors which first attracted him to the Communist movement at a time when many in the Labour Party leadership appeared to be in favour of maintaining the British Empire. By 1924 the Comintern had devolved responsibility for the communist movement in India to the CPGB, and, although Dutt was banned from visiting India himself (and indeed the *Labour Monthly* was banned from sale there), he was closely involved in discussions with people like the revolutionary N.M. Roy on what should be the attitude to such matters as Gandhi's civil disobedience campaign, and to the formation of the Indian National

Congress. During the later thirties he had talks with, among others, the Indian Congress leader, Nehru. There were continuous arguments concerning communist collaboration with nationalist movements and the problems associated with the Hindu-Muslim divide.

For most of the time between the wars, the Communist Party in India was illegal and contact had to be kept under cover. But after the war Dutt was suddenly allowed to visit that country, where he addressed many meetings to which thousands of people came. His book, *India Today* – published in 1940 – is still highly regarded in that country.

Though some people may think that the subtitle to this book is misleading, Callaghan provides a very expert study of a highly controversial character and the political events which influenced him. A book much to be recommended.

Noreen Branson

Noreen Branson is a leading historian of the CPGB and the author of History of the Communist Party of Great Britain 1927–1941.

BUKHARIN'S WRITINGS

Wladislaw Hedeler, editor and compiler, *Nikolai Bukharin: Bibliographie* (Decaton Verlag, Mainz, Germany,1993), DM69.

Nikolai I Bukharin (1888–1938) was one of the leading theoreticians of the Bolshevik party in the first decade after the October Revolution. During the period of the 'New Economic Policy' in Soviet Russia, from 1921 to around 1928, Bukharin provided a theoretical framework to justify the existing political and economic structures and link them to the ultimate goal of a socialist society. His numerous published works ranged from cheap polemics to serious contributions to Marxist theory.

Bukharin fell from favour in the latter part of 1928, when the Stalin faction abandoned its hitherto cautious economic policies in favour of an ambitious programme of investment which relied more on coercive than on economic mechanisms. Bukharin and his close colleagues Alexei Rykov and Mikhail Tomsky were declared to be 'right opportunists' and were removed from the most important of their positions in the Soviet government and Communist International apparatus. This factional struggle extended to the parties of the Communist International, which were instructed by Moscow to root out their own 'right deviationists'. In the British CP, this campaign was used by Harry Pollitt and R. Palme Dutt to marginalise and remove from office certain leading figures from the first decade of the CPGB's history – most notably Albert Inkpin, T.A. Jackson and Andrew Rothstein. In certain other parties, particularly the American, Swedish and German CPs, the factional struggle led to the formation of breakaway organisations, such as the KPD(O) of Heinrich Brandler and August Thalheimer in Germany. These parties opposed the 'Third Period', ultra-revolutionary line adopted by the Communist International after 1929, and sympathised with the defeated Bukharin group.

The ideas of Bukharin enjoyed a brief revival in the USSR in the late 1980s, as the CPSU under Mikhail Gorbachev looked for ideological antecedents for the economic policies of *perestroika*. Vladislaw Hedeler's bibliography is a product of the meeting of the 'old' and 'new' Bukharinism. Decaton Verlag is the publishing house of the descendants of the Brandler group. Hedeler, who started work on his Bukharin bibliography in Moscow in 1983, was greatly assisted by the Bukharin revival and the subsequent opening of the CPSU Central Party Archive and other closed collections in the former USSR and GDR. This has enabled Hedeler to compile a bibliography of 1715 published items, and an appendix listing letters and unpublished documents in the former Central Party Archive's Buin holding.

Hedeler's book, which includes brief introductory and explanatory remarks in German, is a valuable addition to the literature on Bukharin. A pious Bukharin bibliography, published by the American scholar Sidney Heitman in 1969, listed only 937 items, not least because the libraries and archives of the Soviet Union and Eastern Europe remained closed to him. Heitman's work is certainly superseded by Hedeler. Nonetheless, it is unfortunate that Decaton Verlag did not attempt to emulate the much clearer presentation of the Heitman bibliography. This applies particularly to the transliteration system used by Hedeler, which is inconsistent and omits the accents needed to distinguish between certain characters of the Russian alphabet. Since transliteration is intended to assist non-Russian-speakers, this is an avoidable shortcoming in what is otherwise an excellent piece of work.

Francis King

Francis King has written extensively on communist history and worked on the relocation of the CPGB archive.

MAIN ALTERNATIVE?

Ernest Mandel, *Trotsky as Alternative* (Verso, London, 1995), 86pp. ISBN 1 85984 085 X, £13.95.

Ernest Mandel is the foremost postwar international leader of 'orthodox Trotskyism'. For almost half a century he has been one of the principal interpreter's of Trotsky's ideas whether as erudite theoretician in books such as *Marxist Economic Theory* (1962), *Late Capitalism* (1975), *From Stalinism to Eurocommunism* (1978), *Revolutionary Marxism Today* (1979) and *Beyond Perestroika: the Future of Gorbachev's USSR* (1989), or as a political leader of the 'Fourth International'.

In his latest book, Mandel aims to restore 'full justice' to Trotsky after 'seventy years of lies and fifty years of silence'. He wastes no time with the old familiar slanders. Even *Izvestia* published an article on Trotsky, in August 1990, which described him as a 'great and irreproachable revolutionary', the second man in the party and state. Mandel's real target, in this sustained attempt to assess Trotsky's place in the twentieth century, is those 'new myths and accusations' which, while conceding Trotsky's status as a revolutionist-of-action, the organiser of the 1917 Revolution, the creator of the Red Army, deny that he represented a real alternative to Stalin. Beneath their murderous conflict, it is often implied, the two had a deeper identity.

Rejecting this new orthodoxy Mandel makes the bold and controversial claims that: 'Trotsky's theoretical and political achievements are without parallel this century. He will go down in history as the most important strategist of the socialist movement' (p. 10).

Of all the important socialists of the twentieth century it was Trotsky who recognised most clearly the main tendencies of development and the principal contradictions of the epoch and it was Trotsky who gave the clearest formulations to an appropriate emancipatory strategy for the international labour movement (p. 1).

Using the results of historical research on hitherto unavailable archives, Mandel builds his case across chapters dealing not only with what he considers Trotsky's most profound contributions to Marxism – the theory and strategy of Permanent Revolution, the struggle against the degeneration of the Russian Revolution and his theory of Stalinism, and the theory of fascism and the fight for the United Front – but also with Trotsky's views on the National Question, the Jewish question and anti-semitism, the relationship between Party and Class, and even with matters of military strategy and literary criticism. On all these questions Mandel insists Trotsky represented 'the main historical alternative to Stalinism and Social Democracy'.

❏ Trotsky on the market

For example, Mandel tackles the widely held belief that Trotsky's economic policy was 'eventually adopted under Stalin' after 1928, as Eric Hobsbawm puts it in his remarkable tour-de-force, *Age of Extremes*. This view has long underpinned the belief that Trotsky was ultimately no more than a 'Stalinist-without-power'. Using the work of historians Billick, Radzikhovsky, Bordyugov, Koslov and Dainov, Mandel paints a very different picture, of a cautious and moderate Trotsky who offered what Dainov calls a 'civilised Bolshevik model' of economic development in the 1920s. Many readers will be surprised for instance that Trotsky ridiculed the attempt to create a command economy and insisted on the need to use the market in the transition to socialism:

> If a universal mind existed – a mind that could register simultaneously all the processes of nature and society, that could measure the dynamics of their motions, that could forecast the results of their interactions – such a mind, of course, could draw up a faultless and exhaustive economic plan, beginning with the number of acres of wheat down to the last button for a vest. The bureaucracy often imagines that just such a mind is at its disposal; that is why it so easily frees itself from the control of the market and of Soviet democracy. But, in reality, the bureaucracy errs frightfully in the estimate of its spiritual resources … .
>
> The innumerable living participants in the economy, state and private, collective and individual, must serve notice of their needs and of their relative strength not only through the statistical determinations of the plan commission but by the direct pressure of supply and demand. The plan is checked and to a considerable degree realised through the market. … Only through the interaction of these three elements, state planning, the market, and Soviet democracy, can the correct direction of the economy of the transitional epoch be attained. (p. 67)

In 1928 Trotsky denounced Stalin's lurch as 'in breach of the most basic principles of Marxism'. There is no guarantee that Trotsky and

Rakovsky's alternative economic strategy would have worked, of course, but Mandel does demolish the myth that on this question, as on many others, no alternative was proposed. The truly interesting point here is why this obvious fact, available to all in one of Trotsky's most widely accessible books, *The Revolution Betrayed,* was 'forgotten' by so many people, including most Trotskyists. In so far as ideologues shaped this forgetting, one of those most responsible was Mandel himself who painted an often rosy picture of the 'planned economy' of the Soviet Union.

❏ **Not uncritical**

Mandel is far from uncritical of Trotsky, mocking the image of the 'infallible pope' held by many Trotskyist sects. Mandel gives us a Trotsky, for instance, who, alongside the other leading Bolsheviks in the early 1920s, not only supported mistaken authoritarian policies but also provided spurious justifications for abuses of democracy which, although he recovered his democratic balance quickly, would come back to haunt him:

> The Workers Opposition have come out with dangerous slogans. They have made a fetish of democratic principles. They have placed the workers right to elect representatives above the party, as it were, as if the party were not entitled to assert its [sic] dictatorship even if that dictatorship temporarily clashed with the passing moods of the workers democracy. (p. 83)

Mandel also points to Trotsky's 'limited ability to reconcile after a polemic', and to his mistaken belief that the productive forces could not develop under imperialism, an error which produced a failure of strategic response among his supporters after the war, not least Mandel himself, who as late as the 1950s was insisting the crisis was worse than the 1930s!

But ultimately this is a complacent book. Anyone turning to it in hope of some rethinking by a leading Trotskyist after the collapse of communism will be disappointed. Mandel does not address the dilemma posed by the revolutions of 1989 *to orthodox Trotskyists:* how could societies defined as 'workers states', to be defended as qualitatively superior to capitalism, so spectacularly fail to develop either the productive forces or democracy, then collapse amid cheers from those very workers?

The relationship between the historic Trotskyism and Mandel's version of 'post-Trotsky' Trotskyism is at stake here. While Trotsky's views on Stalinism evolved throughout the 1930s, coming close in his last writings, such as his biography of Stalin, to the view that the Soviet Union was a new exploiting society, 'Mandelism' involved a redefinition of Stalinism as part of a mystical 'world revolution', conceived as a demiurge. Trotsky's ideas underwent tortuous 're-interpretation' to rationalise support for Tito, Mao and Castro as the 'blunt instruments' of an Unfolding Historical Process. 'Mandelism' rediscovered for postwar Trotskyism the role vacated by the German dissident communist Heinrich Brandler in the 1930s: the loyal critic of the bureaucracy. As early as 1951 this was all too much for Natalia, Trotsky's widow, who resigned from the 'Fourth International', writing to Mandel enraged at his 'inexcusable idealisation' of Tito, and his general willingness to assign to Stalinism 'a progressive and even a revolutionary role'. These failings she ascribed to his 'obsession by old and outlived formulas', such as the idea that the Soviet Union and its satellites were workers' states because they had nationalised industry. In reply Mandel said Natalia Trotsky was guilty of 'a capitulation under the pressure of Imperialism'. Natalia Trotsky's break was one of a number of figures – Max Shachtman, Hal Draper and Tony Cliff were others – who tried to create a heterodox 'third camp' revolutionary socialism.

This book will certainly force many on the Western European left to question some long held beliefs and prejudices about Trotsky. Mandel ends his book with the ringing declaration 'we are and remain Trotskyists'. But whether Trotsky, amid the rubble of the 'workers' states', would have remained a 'Mandelite' is another question.

Alan Johnson

Alan Johnson is an editor of the magazine Workers Liberty, *and is Head of Contemporary Political Studies at Edge Hill College of Higher Education.*

Since this review was written Ernest Mandel's death has been announced. *Socialist History* **regrets the loss of a renowned theorist and writer in the Marxist tradition.**

REVIEWS

GRAMSCI AFTER EUROCOMMUNISM

Antonio Gramsci, translated and selected by Derek Boothman, *Further Selections from the Prison Notebooks* (Lawrence and Wishart, London, 1995), xxxvii and 618 pp., ISBN 0 8531 5796 0, £45.00 hardback.

Antonio Gramsci, edited and with an introduction by Joseph A. Buttlieg, *Prison Notebooks*, volume one, (Columbia University Press, New York, 1992), xxiii and 608 pp., ISBN 0 2310 6082 3, £29.50 hardback.

Antonio Gramsci, edited by Frank Rosengarten, *Letters from Prison*, volume one, (Columbia University Press, New York, 1994), xxi and 374 pp., ISBN 0 2310 7552 9, £27.50 hardback.

Antonio Gramsci, edited by Frank Rosengarten, *Letters from Prison*, volume two (Columbia University Press, New York, 1994), 431 pp., ISBN 0 2310 7554 5, £27.50 hardback.

Those of Gramsci's prison writings which were popularised in Britain from the early seventies, particularly through Hoare and Nowell-Smith's often reprinted 1971 Lawrence and Wishart selection, proved to be very useful for a significant number of left activists. Readings of the texts on the role of intellectuals, on the nature and forms of exercise of hegemony, and to an increasing degree on Americanism and Fordism, have resourced and underpinned a range of seemingly promising approaches. Strategic work around building progressive alliances and rooting practice in the specific conditions of one's own particular social context was made more sophisticated than it had been through assimilation of some of Gramsci's insights. The importance of cultural questions to effective political strategy was understood by many left intellectuals through a reading of Gramsci, and the development of the whole rich field of cultural studies has been resourced by forms of Gramscianism.

Some of the uses to which Gramsci's suggestive ideas and observations have been applied have taken his students and readers far away from the central concerns which motivated the man himself. This is not in itself a problem. But the very variety and sophistication of Gramsci's thought can tempt us to avoid the question of how the collapse and dissolution of the movement of which he was a leader requires us to recontextualise and reconsider the nature and usefulness of his thought. Whether or not it was explicitly acknowledged, Gramsci's status as a key member of the Italian left and Communist International in the 1920s, and his courage, resilience and resourcefulness in developing a major protect of intellectual work from the prison cell to which Mussolini's men had condemned him to rot, underpinned the status of his work for the Eurocommunists of the 1970s, as did the justified appeal to his role as a founder of their traditions by Europe's most successful and influential non-ruling communist organisation, the PCI.

❏ A distant memory

Though many politicians and intellectuals who are fundamentally shaped by the tradition still have major inputs to make in future, the Eurocommunist project itself is now a distant memory, its key strategies and defining debates making sense only in a historical context which has disappeared. So what is left of Gramsci, now that Eurocommunism, and Soviet communism, and the world which made the Gramsci of the 1930s and his readers of the 1970s, have all gone?

These recent editions of his writings, all very attractively presented, and sensitively and fluently translated, should encourage readers to focus on this question and find their own answers to it. Boothman's selection, a self-conscious successor to Hoare and Nowell-Smith, is a fascinating way into important areas of Gramsci's thought. The theme linking the writings is the investigation of ideology at different levels, and the structures that embody and reproduce it. Nearly 140 pages of selections from the Prison Notebooks on religious thought and movements attest to much more than Gramsci's skill as a tactician in his insistence that, at least in the Italian context, 'the religious tie ought not to constitute an obstacle to working class unity'. Studies on the origin of modern educational principles, and extended considerations on the career and philosophy of Benedetto Croce, all illustrate the extent to which Gramsci's intellectual curiosity and eagerness to explore questions in new ways flourished in the fascist gaol.

It is likely that being imprisoned under Mussolini saved this Marxist intellectual from a fate which would have been even worse, and would have certainly robbed us of the legacy he produced in prison. For his independence of thought and refusal to accept dogmatism and the narrow concerns of those who policed living movements for heresy and insubordination would certainly have brought him into open or hidden conflict with Stalin and the Third International's apparatchiks. Those who carried out these people's orders had more decisive ways of stopping others' brains from functioning than the term of imprisonment which the Italian prosecutor ensured was imposed on Gramsci.

Because the way we have understood Gramsci has centred so much on the ways in which he was an atypical communist leader and intellectual, it is interesting and important that Boothman has given us major chunks of writing on economic questions and on theoretical methodology. Earlier selections from Gramsci showcased the areas of his thought in which he made most distinctive and original contributions, and which were linked to the political debates of the day about political theory and strategy. Boothman complements our awareness of this Gramsci with an implicit reminder that he shared the most orthodox areas of interest for communists and socialists, even if his writings in this area also show 'an original and undogmatic approach, far removed from the mental closure that came to typify the official ideology and authoritarian, bureaucratic political leadership which imposed itself in the former Eastern bloc'.

❑ Saving grace

Boothman's selection, and his stimulating and informative introductions and notes, stand as clear evidence that Gramsci's writings can continue to educate us and open areas of investigation well beyond the contexts within which they were first produced and have since been found useful. They also stand as absolutely essential documents for those who will continue to study one of the most significant political and intellectual figures of the twentieth century. For these reasons, it is to be welcomed that an American publisher has embarked on the important project of producing a complete edition of the Prison Notebooks in English. Columbia's volumes are based on Gerratana's authoritative Italian edition, and the introduction, detailed notes, illustrations and careful descriptions in the first volume convey to the reader not only the contents of these remarkable documents, produced in circumstances of profound personal isolation and political defeat, but also a good sense of the material character of the original manuscripts.

The way in which the notebooks were written and accumulated under the eye of the prison guards, and how they were smuggled out of fascist Italy and protected from suspicious prying eyes during their time in the Soviet Union, makes fascinating reading in itself. Gramsci's achievement is underlined by the understanding of his experience in prison which is conveyed by his letters, also produced in a complete and definitive two-volume set in English by Columbia. Long appreciated as fascinating and moving documents in themselves, as an account of the impact of prison life on one of its victims, for the insights they provide into Gramsci's character and personality and for the suggestive political snippets which punctuate them, the letters leave no doubt that their author was one of twentieth-century communism's saving graces.

Mike Waite

Mike Waite is the Reviews Editor of Socialist History.

BECOMING A FEMINIST-SOCIALIST HISTORIAN

Sally Alexander, *Becoming a Woman and Other Essays in Nineteenth and Twentieth Century Feminist History*, (Virago, London, 1994), 329pp., ISBN 1 85381 750 0, £16.99

Sally Alexander's reputation as an activist in feminist-socialist history is unequalled. As one of the founders of the History Workshop movement and editor of its journal, she was the champion and guide of feminist-socialist history, debating with rigour the central importance of the social and political construction of gender to the development of social class and of social and protest movements. Much of what is now commonplace in accounts of the way gender and class roles developed together in the nineteenth century can be traced back to her inspirational work. Her accessibility, the support she gives students and colleagues, in the workplace, at London history group meetings, at History Workshop and other conferences spring from her commitment to the dissemination of history. An example of the breadth of her activity was a lively, skilled, dramatic address given at an Oxford seminar series in the early 1980s, in the entirely inappropriate, grandly austere setting of the echoing salons of the Victorian Examination Schools: the result was the founding of the Oxford Feminist History Group, the support ground for a generation of feminist historians now working in the academies and editing the journals of the British and international education systems. This reviewer's acquaintance with Sally Alexander is slight, but intimate; she diminished the distance to the metropolitan editors and academics, who still exert the powers of patronage, to a historian then writing in the Wiltshire wilds, discussing her work freely, cooking spaghetti, spreading her cloak over the bad patches.

This welcome edition of Sally Alexander's work is written with the verve, and has the range of content one would expect. Through two hundred years we move amongst ordinary people, their workplaces and their homes, their political meetings, their campaigns of protest, their shopping trips. We see the handloom weaver through contemporary eyes: 'employed at the same time as she is surveying her domestic affairs ... she will leave her loom, peel potatoes for dinner ... should her child cry she will give it the breast ... and return to her loom again' (p. 120). We learn how London women between the wars did their hair and we see their images of glamour. We hear speeches to the crowd, intimate conversations, ordinary people's 'scorn of the rich' (p. 118). And always, we trace the relations between women and men, sexual, political, economic, societal, revealed and reinforced by language delineating the 'proper place' of women. It is Alexander's strength that epistemology and methodology are rigorously linked, that we are given a conceptual framework to understand the historical account, told why a piece of research was important to her and how she undertook it. We are therefore empowered to challenge, invited to debate. The prose is simple and direct; the type large and well spaced (although the binding of my copy was weak). As is unfortunately now common, the footnotes are inconveniently gathered together at the end of the book.

❑ **The semi-covert theme**

Although its range is admirable, one could suggest several alternative arrangements for this anthology. The diffidence about defining and cultivating a central theme is the more disappointing in that one is outlined, but is then allowed to lose itself. The review with Yvonne Kapp, centrally placed, is fascinating for the parallels it reveals between respondent and researcher; the scattered writing and the career changes. It also illuminates the semi-covert theme: how one becomes a writer. What it is that impels a politically committed feminist, supporting a family, working, to devote great chunks of time to the rigours of historical scholarship, why that scholarship is necessary and what are its aims. These points are discussed in the introduction that is one of the best new essays we are given; for instance, 'history has no subject. For me listening to women's speech ... led to a concept of the subject divided by sex and driven by phantasy and the unconscious as well as by economic need' (p. xii); 'Both the oedipal and the aspirant impulses of my feminism are rooted in the contradictions of the 1940s' (p. xiii); 'Men were important to my mother. She had grown up ... in the shadow of the ... Great War' (p. 172). Alexander traces her break with historical materialism and her continuing interest in political economy; how she addressed the imperatives of 'race' and ethnicity; changing feminist demands; 'the exploration of power through image and language' (p. xix); her reading of Lacan, Althusser and Freud; the groups of women with whom she worked. As she inspects the meaning of gender, its historicity, its relationship to economics, psychoanalysis, sexuality, Alexander reflects: 'my personal history is there too in the full-stops and the commas'.

I wanted more of this personal history, was hungry for these issues to be more fully revealed and debated. Alexander tells us: 'I would like to write a history which makes the gap between phantasy and reality more comprehensible.' I want such a work, as Alexander says of Yvonne Kapp's *chef d'oeuvre*, 'a magnificent book, a tour de force';[1] this we will receive, when she shuts her door on clamorous supplicants, such as this reviewer.

Christine Collette

Christine Collette teaches at Edge Hill University College.

NOTES

1. Yvonne Kapp, *Eleanor Marx: volume I, Family Life 1855–1883; volume II, The Crowded Years 1884–1898* (Lawrence and Wishart, 1972, 1976); (2 vols, Virago, 1979).

RECLAIMING HISTORY

Jerry Rothwell, ed., *Creating Meaning: A Book About Culture and Democracy* (Valley & Vale, Blaengarw, 1992), 82pp., £6.50.

The study of local history is a growing activity. Much academic work is relevant to current concerns, but is not easily accessible to ordinary citizens, generally involved as individuals rather than as representatives of a community; the output tends to be antiquarian and without contemporary significance. By contrast, a community arts group in South Wales has been trying for ten years to help local people reclaim their history as a tool for struggling for a better life.

This softcover book is Valley & Vale's most recent publication, based on articles describing and evaluating some of their work. The linking theme is the belief that any advance of democracy means that people must take a hand in creating the culture that defines their identities.

The group's efforts to broaden participation in dance, drama, music, design and video through workshops, projects and products have led to a growing emphasis on local history as a central feature of community culture. Activity on pressing issues, such as innovative posters and an exhibition during the 1984–88 miners' strike, remains detached and discontinuous unless it is put in a long-term context. So among the group's publications are *The Valleys Autobiography: A People's History of the Garw, Llynfi and Ogmore Valleys* and *In Our Own Words, In Our Own Pictures*, a history of Barry, both with parallel video-exhibitions. Underlying their approach is the view that ' ... oral history has been seen primarily as a resource for historians ... It has rarely been seen as a resource for those whose experience it uses.'

Valley & Vale are rightly proud of their achievement in refurbishing the historic but neglected Workmen's Hall & Institute in Blaengarw as one of their centres, a project to which local people made a significant input during planning as well as implementation.

Aware of the danger that local history may remain parochial, the group has drawn on experiences of community arts in Mexico and China, and put on a festival bringing together artists from South Wales and South Africa. This was an opportunity to show how the destinies of the two peoples are linked in concrete ways. For instance, the sale of an existing steel plant and the import of South African coal 'indicate a clear relationship between the low wages and poor working conditions in South Africa and growing unemployment in Wales'.

The last essay in the book tellingly sets Valley & Vale's approach against three multi-million pound cultural events of 1992: the Ebbw Vale Garden Festival, EuroDisney and the Seville Universal Exposition. All distort history in order to conceal conflict and suppress struggle.

No doubt it is an easier task to involve people in recovering and using local history in isolated and close-knit Welsh mining valleys, or in Barry, with its rapid rise and fall as a coal port, than in the more polyglot and changeful communities in which most British people live. Valley & Vale are well aware that their work won't make much difference to the future of our people unless it helps others to do likewise in more demanding contexts. Though its conclusions are marred by some wordy generalisations, this book – especially when supplemented by some of the group's more specific publications – is a remarkable document. It can surely inspire anybody seeking to help a community or an organisation to refashion and take hold of its history, and make good use of it in shaping struggles for greater democracy.

David Grove

AN INCOMPLETE PICTURE

Desmond Graham, edited with an introduction, *Poetry of the Second World War: An International Anthology* (Chatto & Windus, London, 1995), xxi & 295 pp., ISBN 0 7011 6299 6, £18.99.

The editor of this anthology has undertaken a massive task: to bring together poems from many countries and languages which convey the experience of living through the Second World War. It contains 244 poems by 130 poets from some 20 countries, over three-fifths of them translations from French, German, Spanish, Italian, Gaelic, Czech, Polish, Hungarian, Romanian, Bulgarian, Greek, Russian, Yiddish, Japanese and other languages. The standard of translation is remarkably high; only a few of the translations do not read as good English poems in their own right. Many aspects of the war are covered: premonitions of its coming, life in the forces, the blitz, the fighting in Western Europe, North Africa and Russia, the war at sea and in the air, resistance movements, exile, the plight of the refugees, prison camps, forced labour, the Holocaust, Hiroshima, victory and liberation.

Every reader will find much of value in this book, whether their interest is primarily in poetry or in the war. Although some of the poems by British writers are old anthology favourites, there are still discoveries to be made among the poems by English-language writers, and still more among the translations, which reveal many unfamiliar aspects of the war. An outstanding example is the poems of the Hungarian Jew Miklos Radnoti, which are well represented. Already a well-known poet before the war, he was conscripted into a forced labour battalion and finally shot, yet even in appalling conditions he managed to write poems in which, while concealing nothing of the suffering and degradation surrounding him, he could still give poignant expression to his hopes and aspirations.

Despite its many positive qualities, however, this anthology succeeds only in part in its avowed intention of 'conveying the vast and terrible sweep of the war'. One reason for its partial failure is that the editor sees the war almost exclusively through Western eyes. The anthology is planned, for example, on the assumption that the Second World War began with the German invasion of Poland. In fact, it originated as two separate wars, in Asia and in Europe, merging into one with Pearl Harbour and the German declaration of war on the United States. Either 7 July 1937 or 7 December 1941 is a tenable date for the beginning of the Second World War, 1 September 1939 is not.

❏ Imbalance

This is not a mere quibble. The fact that Graham makes 1939 his starting-point is symptomatic of the way in which he ignores almost completely the part played in the war by the Asian peoples. China was at war longer than any of the other Allied countries, and lost several times as many soldiers and civilians killed as the British Commonwealth, France and the United States put together, yet not a line by a Chinese poet appears in the book. Over two million Indian troops fought in the war, but there is nothing by Indian poets. Although 372,000 Africans served in the British forces, there is no African verse. The peoples of North Africa, the Middle East and Southeast Asia are equally ignored. The non-European languages, in fact, are represented solely by translations from Japanese. The editor of such an anthology is admittedly dependent on the availability of translations, but it is difficult to believe that no good translations of Chinese, Indian, Arabic or African war poems exist.

Another disturbing feature of this anthology is its failure to bring out the heroic nature of the struggle of the peoples of Europe, Asia and the United States against two of the most evil regimes in history. Its exclusion of Chinese and Southeast Asian verse and its inclusion of several poems on Hiroshima leaves the impression that the Japanese were more sinned against than sinning. The infamy of Nazism is fully documented; in particular, a whole section of the book is devoted to poems on the Holocaust, some of them almost unbearably painful. Although it could be questioned whether they have any place in an anthology of war poetry, the editor was certainly right to include them, for nothing could illustrate more clearly the nature of the evil against which the Allies were fighting. The selection of poems, however, lays more emphasis on the evil than on the struggle against it. W.B. Yeats defended his exclusion of Wilfred Owen's poems from *The Oxford Book of Modern Verse* with the assertion that 'passive suffering is not a theme for poetry', but in Graham's anthology passive suffering is a major theme. Even combatants appear in it more often as sufferers than as fighters, with the result that the book lacks balance.

❑ Poetry and Resistance

The First World War taught us to distrust heroics written by poets at a safe distance from the fighting. There is only one example of such verse in this book, Allen Tate's *Ode to Our Young Pro-consuls of the Air*, a poem so bad that one wonders whether it was meant for burlesque. Distrust of heroics, however, does not necessarily exclude tributes to heroism, what John Manifold called, in an eloquent poem not included in this anthology, 'courage chemically pure'. One form of heroism especially is almost ignored; the resistance movements are represented by only five poems (two Bulgarian, two Polish and one Yugoslav), compared with 30 on the Holocaust. There is nothing from such French and Italian Resistance poets as Aragon, Eluard and Fortini except one poem by Aragon which does not deal with the resistance. Graham attempts to justify his omission of their verse with the feeble excuse that it was 'coded' and therefore 'rarely reads well' in translation. I suspect that the real reason why he gave the resistance so little space is that throughout Europe and Southeast Asia it was largely organised and led by communists, and many of its poets were communist or other left-wingers. By playing down the contribution of the resistance to the defeat of fascism, and ignoring that of the Asian and African peoples, this anthology gives an incomplete and even a distorted picture of the war.

Charles Hobday

GOSSIP MADE THE WORLD GO ROUND

Melanie Tebbutt, *Women Talk? A Social History Of 'Gossip' in Working-Class Neighbourhoods1880–1960* (Scolar Press, Aldershot, 1995), 206 pp., ISBN 1 85928 026 9, £35 hardback.

Idle, ribald, inconsequential, girly gossip is the slippery stuff of this study of working-class women's history. Forgotten chitchat and long-dead scandal are resurrected from a variety of sources – autobiography, press reports, popular literature and, importantly, oral testimony – to illustrate Tebbut's thesis that gossip played a complex, yet formative, part in shaping working-class social values over the 80-year period that her research spans. Gossiping, says Tebbutt, was instrumental in defining the communities where it was generated.

According to social science literature, a good gossip entails exchanging information about other people who are mutually known. But equally, there are definitions from a veritable academy of researchers on the subject – anthropologists, behavioural psychologists, linguists – all of which Tebbutt draws on in the course of her work. This means, of course, that although this book is presented as history, it has an interdisciplinary edge. Where the research crosses disciplinary boundaries it is at its most illuminating – but casting so much new light must have given Tebbut something of a headache in terms of containability. Perhaps that also reflects the subject matter. Picture a volume battling to close its covers on an octavo of hot gossip and interesting tangents. Clearly a case of women's talk causing trouble.

❏ The gossiping housewife myth

As Dale Spender has pointed out, women's conversation has traditionally been disparaged as an inferior form of talk. In addition, as a print culture emerged in the eighteenth and nineteenth centuries, largely excluding women's words, there was a further implicit downgrading of their oral culture which became associated with superstition and ignorance. Chattering, nattering, prattling – silly, superficial modes of talk – these are all feminine forms of speech. Men, on the other hand, discuss, or debate. Did they ever gossip? Not in the contemporary literature, anyway. Understandably then, there isn't much space for man talk in this book. When men feature here, they are slinking in and out of their houses, on their way home from work, on their way to the pub. They are uncomfortable, alien creatures, almost entirely marginal to the culture of the streets and housing estates that they nominally inhabit.

The Tebbutt-version street is pretty much a women-only affair, featuring aprons, net curtains and a mandatory matriarch. But the idle gossiping housewife is absent here – the women who inhabit Tebbut's landscape work phenomenally hard, measuring their achievements against a gossip-sustained yardstick. Only when housework was finished, in fact, would women gather at their doorsteps to talk, conscious that showing their face too early of an afternoon meant they hadn't paid due attention to the cleaning. Otherwise, gossip was conducted in snatches, on the way to the corner shop, or laundering at the wash-house. Imagine a patchwork of domestic chores, stitched together with women's words – the fabric of community. Could it be that gossip was the making of the English working classes?

❏ A portrait of working-class women's lives

What makes *Women Talk* a delightful, rather than simply an insightful read, are the oral testimonies and recollections that Tebbutt uses to service her broader analyses. Fragments of half-remembered conversation emerge from the text in a re-enactment of another way of life. History and narrative come together to provide a portrait of, rather than just a discourse on, women in working-class communities.

This is illustrated nowhere better than in an attempt to pin down the way that gossip informed a collective morality, sprung from the need to survive under trying conditions. In order to establish the precise tenets of this morality, we are treated to 35 pages of *actual gossip*. I can't pass any on right now, of course. What I can tell you is that Tebbutt successfully avoids the likely pitfalls of using I-said-to-her-and-she-said-to-me as evidence, by placing her amassed gossip firmly in the context of ideas about the family and its role in the urban community. Anyway, there are some engrossing anecdotes here.

❑ The privatiation of talk

In the latter part of *Women Talk* the scene shifts away from the street and onto the housing estates that sprung up, between the wars, as poorer housing was cleared. In some sense at least, the gossip stopped here. Life on the estates was less about mutually-reliant neighbours than about the self-enclosed family unit whose respectability was based on self-sufficiency. Popping in for a cuppa became more difficult than it had been hitherto, as some women protected their slum-antithesis, hard-won, private space from casual callers. Instead, says Tebbutt, by the 1960s women began to watch their gossip on television, as soaps like Coronation Street emerged. Hilda Ogden, Vera Duckworth, Ena Sharples and the rest mirrored, albeit in stereotype, some of the speech habits that working-class women had developed.

Women Talk has given Hilda Ogden and co. a real-life family tree. More importantly, so much of a genealogy that was sparsely populated or indistinct has been restored by Tebbut's painstaking research. Working-class women had a history all along, of course. This book is in the best tradition of tell-it-like-it-was.

Karen Triggs

Karen Triggs teaches in the Social Science department at Richmond-Upon-Thames College, Twickenham.

GALLOWS HUMOUR

F.K.M. Hillenbrand, *Underground Humour in Nazi Germany 1933–1945* (Routledge, London, 1995), 297pp., ISBN 0 4150 9785, £45 hardback

This is a serious book about humour, painstakingly compiled by F.K.M. Hillenbrand, a witness to the developing chaos in Germany which led to the Second World War. At £45 the price may seem a bit steep, but it is not really a coffee table book to be dipped into, rather an academic document which attempts to collect many examples of underground humour in Germany between 1933 and 1945 before it disappears for ever. Humour has always been an integral ingredient of any culture and as a working stand-up comic, I feel the political and social climate in which a country finds itself has always been an important ingredient of that humour. In Britain, many people feel under siege, owing to the uncaring attitude of the present government. This is reflected in the work of several comedians working on the comedy circuit, although a stronger attitude was seen in the 1980s when Mrs Thatcher was doing her worst. However, the personalities and foibles of all our politicians are very good fodder for jokes.

I think that the darker and more tragic the circumstances in a society, the stronger and more risque the humour becomes. I have a brother who is married to a German woman and having travelled to Germany many times I can feel the shame and guilt that still exists, particularly among younger people, about the terrible things that took place under Hitler. Many Germans still find it hard to admit what happened. I recently gave my brother a collection of the *Fawlty Towers* video tapes and he says he can still not bring himself to show 'The Germans' to his father-in-law. However, many people in the Germany of the 1930s and 1940s used humour to defend themselves, in a small way, against what was happening.

F.K.M Hillenbrand has divided this book into chapters covering all aspects of the era, including personalities of the Third Reich, the Jews and the war itself. Each page is peppered with notes and at times it becomes quite a chore turning constantly to the back, discouraging the not-so-serious reader. There is a wealth of jokes about the different personalities who were part of Hitler's Third Reich, all pertaining to the most identifiable aspect of the individual's personality. The author gives us a full description, for example, of Goering and then goes on to illustrate this with jokes. Some of the material he has collected is not what we know as 'jokes' and seem to be rather snatches of conversation, but many do take traditional and recognisable joke form: 'Hitler, Goebbels and Goring have at last been brought to the gallows. Goering turns to Goebbels and remarks, "I always told you that the issue would finally be settled in the air."'

F.K.M. Hillenbrand has steered clear of the more sick or sexual jokes, remarking at one point that a joke is too 'scabrous' to warrant inclusion in the book. I think it is wrong in a serious book of this nature that he felt it necessary to do this. The appalling situation in which many people found themselves, I feel could only be expressed in very strong terms, although I understand that he may have wished to avoid sensationalism.

The section about the Jews is a tragic read, underlining the desperation many people felt in trying to escape the tentacles of Hitler's

Aryan laws. It also illustrates the lengths many Jews went to to hide their roots. One of my favourites in the book illustrates this, combined with a hatred of Hitler.

A Jew appears at a register office with an urgent request to be permitted to change his name. The official seems very reluctant at first but eventually asks the Jew his name.
'My name is Adolf Stinkfoot.'
'Well,' says the official, 'in that case I think I can accede to your request. Which new name have you chosen?'
'Maurice Stinkfoot.'

There is a very interesting section on women. Hitler always had a very flawed relationship with women which is reflected in the attitude of the Third Reich towards them. In a newspaper of the time: 'The most unnatural thing we can encounter in the streets is a German woman, who, disregarding all laws of beauty, has painted her face with oriental war paint.' Sadly there were not many women comics around to counter this article.

There is also a chapter in the book on the Third Reich as seen by others, including a short section on British humour. This is not as long as I would have liked it, but you can't have everything.

Having covered 'Hitler's War', we are brought to the aftermath of the war and the scramble by many former Nazis to distance themselves.

> In '33 all hale and hearty
> Most eagerly we joined the Party
> Then, making profits all the way,
> 'Heil Hitler' all of us would say.
> Divine he seemed to high and low
> But were we Nazis? Never! No!

I think this is a very valuable book which has dealt in a very thoughtful way with a difficult, tragic, area. Not only does it cover well all the humour, but explains in a very clear way the development of the Nazi party and how the various members of Hitler's staff behaved. If you've got £45 to spare, buy it.

Jo Brand

Jo Brand frequently appears on television.

IN BRIEF – AUTOBIOGRAPHICAL WRITING

John Gorman's autobiography *Knocking Down Ginger* (Caliban Books, London, 1995), 260 pages, ISBN 1 8506 6018 2, £16.50 hardback) takes the familiar form of tracing the author's life from a poor working-class childhood through to politicisation and the early stages of a successful career. Gorman's portrayal of London's east end in the 1930s, the accounts of his friendship with Lionel Bart as the two young men struggled to build up their design and printing company, and his involvement in the Communist Party from 1949 to 1956, give structure to a book stuffed with entertaining anecdote and an eye for telling detail.

Caliban Books already boast a respected list of autobiographical writing from the eighteenth and nineteenth centuries. It is to be hoped that Gorman's book will be one of many solicited from living working-class activists. Perhaps they will also encourage Gorman to continue his story from 1956 – his activity after he left the CPGB has included involvement in CND and the Committee of 100, Labour Party membership and a major contribution to the study of the visual history of the British labour movement – many readers will know his work *Banner Bright*.

John Harrison's *Scholarship Boy: A Personal History of the Mid-Twentieth Century* (Rivers Oram, London, 1995), 192 pages, ISBN 1 8548 9072 7, £16.95 hardback) is equally well written, and traces the author's rather different life through the same period. Harrison makes the point that 'unlike the working class, whose history has been enthusiastically recovered by several generations of labour and socialist historians, the lower-middle classes still await a devoted chronicler ... perhaps the time has come to rescue them from the enormous condescension of intellectuals and literati'. Though he sometimes is a little bogged down in his detailed treatment of family relationships, Harrison charts his course through education, war service and his career as an increasingly respected historian in a way which often generates wider and interesting insights into social life. His account of how education provided an escape route for a youth frustrated with what he perceived as the constraints of a narrow and limiting background raises a consideration about how much autobiographical writing from left activists and intellectuals tends to trace how they became different and to some extent cut off from their fellows – a phenomenon which Victor

Kiernan has recently linked to the problem of anti-intellectualism in the Labourist tradition.

The problem of atypical voices being the ones which convey the experience particularly of working-class life is offset to some extent by studies which integrate a considerable volume of varied writing and oral material from 'ordinary' people. John Burnett's *Idle Hands: The Experience of Unemployment 1790–1990* (Routledge, London, 1994), 368 pages, ISBN 0 4150 5501 6, £12.99 paperback) coveys the cruel reality of a wide variety of forms of unemployment by drawing from over 200 memoirs, unpublished manuscripts and collections of letters. The limitations of simply collecting the expressions of subjective experience are overcome by Burnett's impressive, if somewhat dry, analysis. The balance of analysis and autobiographical writing is different in two classic collections edited and introduced by Burnett, which have been reissued to coincide with the publication of *Idle Hands*. In *Useful Toil: Autobiographies of Working People from the 1820s to the 1920s* (Routledge, London, 1994 – originally Allen Lane 1974), 352 pages, ISBN 0 4151 0399 1, £12.99 paperback) and in *Destiny Obscure: Autobiographies of Childhood, Education and Family from the 1820s to the 1920s* (Routledge, London 1994 – originally Allen Lane 1982), 367 pages, ISBN 0 4151 0401 7, £12.99 paperback), Burnett restricts himself to an introductory chapter and to endnotes and commentary on the remarkable texts he has chosen and in some cases discovered. All these books remind us that the history of all aspects of social life is also the history of real individuals striving to live and make sense of their lives.

MW

BOOKS RECEIVED

Reviews of some of the following are in preparation and will appear in future issues of the journal. Publishers are urged to send items to be considered for review to the editorial team. Readers interested in reviewing any of the publications listed here are invited to contact the editorial team.

Theodor W. Adorno, edited and with an introduction by Stephen Crook, *The Stars Come Down to Earth and other Essays on the Irrational in Culture* (Routledge, London, 1994), 176 pages, ISBN 0 4151 0568, £12.99 pbk.

Geoff Andrews, Nina Fishman and Kevin Morgan, eds, *Opening the Books: Essays on the Social and Cultural History of the British Communist Party* (Pluto Press, London, 1995), ix & 275 pages, ISBN 0 7453 0872 4, £14.95 pbk.

Francis Beckett, *Enemy Within: the Rise and Fall of the British Communist Party* (John Murray, London, 1995), 256 pages, ISBN 0 7195 5310 5, £19.99 hbk.

J.M. Bernstein, *Recovering Ethical Life: Jurgen Habermas and the Future of Critical Theory* (Routledge, London, 1995), xii & 249 pages, ISBN 0 4151 1783 8, £13.99 pbk.

Hans Bertens, *The Idea of the Postmodern; a History* (Routledge, London, 1994), ix & 284 pages, ISBN 4150 6012 5, £12.99 pbk.

Carl Boggs, *The Socialist Tradition: From Crisis to Decline* (Routledge Revolutionary Thought/Radical Movements series, London, 1995), xii & 287 pages, ISBN 0 4159 0670 9, £12.99 pbk.

Stephen Brooke, *Reform and Reconstruction: Britain After the War, 1945–1951* (Manchester University Press, Manchester, 1995), xi & 159 pages, ISBN 0 7190 4505 3, £10.99.

Levon Chorbajian, Patrick Donabedian and Claude Mutafian, *The Caucasian Knot: The History and Geo-Politics of Nagorno-Karabagh* (Zed Books, Politics in Contemporary Asia Series, volume ten, London, 1995), xvi & 198 pages, ISBN 1 8564 9288 5, £14.95 pbk.

Anna Clark, *The Struggle for the Breeches: Gender and the Making of the British Working Class* (Rivers Oram Press, London, 1995), xv & 416 pages, ISBN 1 8548 9075 1, £25.00 hbk.

Ralph Darlington, *The Dynamics of Workplace Unionism: Shop Stewards' Organization in Three Merseyside Plants* (Mansell Publishing Limited, London, 1994), x & 323 pages, ISBN 0 7201 2239 2, £18.99 pbk.

BOOKS RECEIVED

Jim Fyrth, editor, with an introduction by Victor Kiernan, *Labour's Promised Land? Culture and Society in Labour Britain 1945–1951* (Lawrence and Wishart, London, 1995), xv & 320 pages, ISBN 0 8531 5811 8, £16.99 pbk.

Peter Huber, *Stalins Schatten in die Schweiz* (Chronos Verlag, Zurich, 1994), 611 pages, ISBN 3 905311 29 1.

Harvey Klehr, John Earl Haynes and Fridrikh Irgorevich Flrsov, *The Secret World of American Communism* (Yale University Press, Annals of Communism Series, London, 1995), xxxii & 348 pages, ISBN 0 3000 6183 8, £16.95 hbk.

Stephen Koch, *Double Lives: Stalin Willi Munzenberg and the Seduction of the Intellectuals* (Harper Collins, London, 1995), xii & 419 pages, ISBN 0 0025 5516 6, £20.00 hbk.

Richard Lamb, *The Macmillan Years 1957–1963: The Emerging Truth* (John Murray, London, 1995), xi & 245 pages, ISBN 0 7195 5392 X, £25.00 hbk.

Lars T. Lih, Oleg V. Naumov and Olg V. Khlevniuk, eds, *Stalin's Letters to Molotov* (Yale University Press, Annals of Communism Series, London, 1995), xviii & 276 pages, ISBN 0 3000 6211 7, £16.95 hbk.

Bernd Magnus and Stephen Cullenberg, eds, *Whither Marxism? Global Crises in International Perspective* (Routledge, London, 1995), xxiii & 253 pages, ISBN 0 4519 1043 9, £12.99 pbk.

David Margolies and Maroula Joannou, eds, *Heart of the Heartless World: Essays in Cultural Resistance in Memory of Margot Heinemann* (Pluto Press, London, 1995), xiii & 239 pages, ISBN 0 7453 0982 8, £14.95 pbk.

Denis Pye, *Fellowship is Life: The National Clarion Cycling Club. 1895–1995* (Clarion Publishing, Bolton, 1995), vii & 92 pages, ISBN 0 9525 0710 2, £4.95 pbk, from 34 Temple Road, Halliwell, Bolton, Lancashire, BL1 3LT.

Edward Roux, *S.P. Bunting: A Political Biography* (new edition edited and introduced by Brian Bunting, with a foreword by Chris Hani) (Mayibuye Books, Belville, South Africa, 1993), 200 pages, ISBN 1 8680 8162 1.

Jon Simons, *Foucault and the Political* (Routledge, London, 1995), vii & 152 pages, ISBN 0 4151 0066 6, £10.99 pbk.

Berry Lane Corner
Apsley Guise
Milton Keynes MK17 8HZ

Dear Editor

Some of your readers may know that I have been working for the past eight years on a life of John Gollan. It is now almost complete.

Clearly such a book will not be profit-making in the market sense, but some friends have, unsolicited, offered several hundred pounds to help defray the cost of publication.

I wonder whether any of your readers would like to add their names to my list of guarantors? At this stage it would not be more than a declaration of intent, but I should be grateful to receive such a declaration from anyone who is interested.

Yours sincerely

Margot Kettle.

JOIN THE SOCIALIST HISTORY SOCIETY

The Socialist History Society is the heir to a long tradition of Marxist historical study, associated with many eminent historians of the left and marked by regular publications, including over eighty monographs. The work of our members, past and present, has had a far-reaching effect on the perception and teaching of history.

Although the scope of the society is not confined to the recent past, we are especially concerned with labour and democratic history and with the history of women's and black movements. In particular we aim to contribute to an understanding of the history of socialist and revolutionary movements in the twentieth century, to understand both their failures and achievements.

The Society is registered with the Democratic Left but is open to everyone interested in its aims, irrespective of their political or other affiliations. Activities include regular historical discussions and meetings, assistance to researchers, and publications.

Members are entitled to participate in all the Society's activities and be elected to its committee and offices. Membership includes subscription to *Socialist History* without further payment, a very considerable saving.

Annual subscription for individuals is £15 waged, £10 unwaged, and £25 for overseas members.

Send subscription with name and address to:

Secretary,
Socialist History Society,
6, Cynthia Street,
London N1 9JF

Institutional and library subscription is £25 per annum. Send requests to:

Sales Dept
Pluto Press,
345 Archway Road,
London N6 5AA.

EDITORIAL CORRESPONDENCE

Please address all editorial correspondence and copies of books for review to Willie Thompson at Glasgow Caledonian University, Dept of Social Sciences, Cowcaddens Road, Glasgow G4 0BA.

ADVERTISING

For details contact the Marketing Manager, Pluto Press, 345 Archway Road, London N6 5AA (tel 0181 348 2724).

REPORTS

NORTHERN MARXIST HISTORIANS

The Northern Marxist Historians Group founded by John Saville had its most recent twice-yearly meeting in Manchester on 20 September, with thirty to forty people in attendance. In view of the focus of this meeting, its interest to our readers and its relationship to the theme of this number, *Socialist History* feels that it is appropriate to report at some length.

Three papers were presented, all concerned with one aspect or another of history and postmodernism. The first was by John Saville himself and had as its subject the historian of the nineteenth century working class, Gareth Stedman Jones, whose theoretical trajectory from Marxism to postmodernism is emblematic of a highly important trend in current historiography.

John Saville on Gareth Stedman Jones

John Saville opened by noting that the most significant thing about Stedman Jones' writings is the status acquired by his piece 'Rethinking Chartism' in the volume *Languages of Class*, published in 1983. Any historian in the field now feels obliged to quote it, whether favourably or otherwise, and in consequence it has now been extensively discussed, although Stedman Jones hasn't responded to the various critiques which have been directed at it.

In John Saville's view, 'Rethinking Chartism' suffers from two major weaknesses. The first is the emphasis on Chartist *discourse* at the expense of the other dimensions of the movement, and it is indeed this aspect which has been the principal target of the critiques. The other is the question of the nature of the nineteenth century British state, which is left almost entirely out of the discussion.

A historian of militantly postmodernist persuasion, Patrick Joyce (see below) has applauded Stedman Jones' approach, although Joyce actually agrees with the criticisms of its formalistic character. His main reservation however is that Stedman Jones doesn't take far enough his dissolution of class into a pattern of linguistic constructs.

John Saville sketched the outline of Stedman Jones' argument, which runs as follows:

Stedman Jones' argument

A language of political radicalism began to develop in Britain from around the middle of the eighteenth century, reaching maturity in the 1790s under the impact of the French Revolution. Its main focus was upon corruption, abuses in the institutions of church, state, law, corporate and municipal bodies. In this form it was able to provide a vocabulary of grievances for variant forms of radical groups, and increasingly, as Stedman Jones accepts, it became the property of the emergent working class. However the way in which he defines the language of radicalism means that it was such as not to bring about a restructuring of social consciousness. Stedman Jones argues that the use of the concept of *property* was central to the development of the languages of class. The language of radicalism stretched *property* to incorporate the situation of the unpropertied working class – which was a suitable oppositional strategy for the 1830s, but not the 1840s on account of the development of class relationships during the intervening years.

To continue the argument: the political radicalism of the 1790s became plebeian radicalism with a revolutionary edge, but its essential core of meaning did not change to take account of changing class relations. Malthus from the right and Robert Owen from the left were offset by the continuation of the old radical discourse.

This is what Stedman Jones asks us to accept – that the core meaning of radicalism did not alter from the 1790s to the 1840s. The ideology remained isolated from the development of events. We must note the ferment of ideas and events in that half-century; the character of the development of working-class organisations and press – but according to Stedman Jones these had no influence on the meaning of radicalism.

Critique

John Saville developed a comprehensive critique of this position. He is confident that radical understanding over the period did develop from an attack on 'old corruption' to a basic understanding of capitalistic exploitation – witness the use of terms such as 'millocracy' or 'shopocrats'.

With reference to Stedman Jones' contention that Chartism failed to understand a change in the character of the British state in the 1840s towards less repressive modes – he quotes Peel as wanting to remove material causes of popular discontent and stop identifying the state with any particular class faction – John Saville responded that Stedman Jones doesn't refer to the significance of the 1832 Reform Act and the sharing of power it implied between the aristocracy and the bourgeoisie, the former continuing to command central government and the latter entrenched in the boroughs by the Municipal Corporations Act of 1835. In 1848, the year of Chartism's suppression, the Whigs, the bourgeois-inclined aristocratic faction, were in office and their bourgeois allies controlled every corporation apart from Liverpool. Even more striking is the absence of any reference to the tumultuous history of Chartism in the 1840s, nor the active and widespread repression to which it was subjected.

John Saville went on to criticise the notion that a fundamental change in the class outlook of government was taking place during the 1840s. The Mines Act of 1842 was a piece of upper-class philanthropy carried by a parliament shocked at revelations of the conditions existing in that industry. It had almost nothing to do with the Ten-Hour agitation.

The financial reforms of the 1842 Budget, the Limited Liability Act of 1844, the Bank Charter Act of the same year and Corn Law repeal in 1846 did not amount to a coherent programme which sustains the weight of analysis that Stedman Jones lays upon it. Nor does he refer to the influence of the French revolutionary thought on the Chartist revival of 1847–48, nor to developments in Ireland, nor to the near-insurrectionary movement in the north of England (associated with Irish developments) nor finally to the total mobilisation of the state's coercive forces in response to these trends.

In conclusion John Saville raised some general questions and observations:

1. The significance of language and discourse has admittedly been neglected by left historians in the past – but not altogether. Edward Thompson has drawn attention to the strange demise of the Ricardian or Smithian socialist tradition of the earlier part of the nineteenth century and asked the question why there was no second generation developing their conceptual framework in the 1830 and 1840s.
2. Why was there no further development of Owenism when the background conditions were so propitious?
3. Why did Chartism die away so quickly?

He suggested a number of answers. Repression and persecution can't be discounted. The mass of jail sentences passed on the movement's second-rank and middle-level organisers may have been comparatively short, but they were disabling and liable to be renewed after release if the victim again offended politically. Moreover, the previous insurrectionary centres were absent in 1848.

An ideological dimension has also to be taken into account. Free-market notions were spreading and penetrating the public consciousness, An increase of racism (mostly anti-Irish) was occurring in the context of declining radicalism. Economic developments were opening up opportunities for skilled workers, and the amalgamated unions were not far in the future. Very quickly Chartism became a memory of the past – indeed at astonishing speed – or turned into myth by Charles Kingsley and other novelists.

In sum, he concluded, this renowned article is so full of inadequacies that it becomes pretty well useless for anyone aiming at a revisionist account of nineteenth century working-class history to use as a peg on which to hang their case.

Discussion
In the discussion which followed the paper it was pointed out that Stedman Jones' work had become a statement of the primacy of politics and political language against materialist analysis. It must be acknowledged he had thereby supplemented our previous understanding, but the quarrel with Stedman Jones is that he wants his own interpretation not to supplement but to displace that understanding. Another participant referred to the terror into which the British ruling class was thrown by the French Revolution of February 1848 and to a circumstance which had been absent in 1839 – the convergence in that year of Chartist and Irish radicalism. The Irish sent a delegation to revolutionary Paris. The ruling class had adopted a very calculated measure of repression, very severe in breadth, but aimed, with the memory of Peterloo in mind, to avoid bloodshed if at all possible.

Neville Kirk on Patrick Joyce
Neville Kirk presented the second paper, an extensive critique of a historian fully and uncompromisingly committed to a postmodernist approach – Patrick Joyce. Joyce is an enormously prolific and influential historian whose central preoccupation has been with the question of class consciousness. Joyce's work is not without its merits.

He has drawn attention to the importance of culture in the construction of social reality, and more specifically to the different kinds of consciousness that labouring people held in the nineteenth century.

There is much however that is less convincing:

1. Underestimation of the influence of class, particularly in relation to the first half of the ninteenth century.
2. He skips over important discontinuities in popular consciousness and discourse between the second and third quarters of that century, and appears to imagine that he personally invented these debates.
3. In relation to method he is very partial and selective – he fails to engage with awkward evidence.
4. His epistemology aims to subvert the difference between representations of reality and the real and thereby loses the dialogue between concept and evidence. 'Proof' becomes highly problematic.

In *Work, Society and Politics* (1980) Joyce developed the thesis that the decline of Chartism and the growth of industrialisation was followed in Lancashire by paternalism, deferentiality and loss of class consciousness. Dependency grew on the employer as a provider of work and such dependency was not forced, but internalised and accepted by the workforce. The argument represents a direct challenge to Marx with its emphasis on consciousness as against material situation as the historical determinant and is antagonistic to a Marxian class analysis. Joyce claims that historians have exaggerated the degree of conflict between employers and workers. In fact Joyce has now disowned this text, regarding it as insufficiently discourse-orientated.

The discontinuity from *Work, Society and Politics* that has been revealed with his subsequent writing is that he has severed the links between reality and external agency and adopted the position that there is no reality external to discourse. His criticisms of Marx and the concept of class are becoming more strident – he is saying in effect that social class is not all that important but that subjectivity is, and he is ambiguous regarding the agency of historical actors.

In fact Joyce has come to adopt the central tenets of the New Cambridge school of historians, especially Stedman Jones. These assert that the continuities in nineteenth century radicalism overshadow the discontinuities, and therefore hold that the transition from Chartism to the labour consciousness of the later ninteenth century is not problematic, nor is the subsequent birth of the Labour Party. We have to be clear that these are important arguments that need to be taken seriously.

They greatly devalue the importance of class, arguing that politics and political ideas and language are what matter most in history. Thus *liberalism* is the most important influence in the history of Britain – and of the US.

It is necessary to recognise that, though these debates are important, they're not particularly new, above all that on working-class identity. The same incidentally is true regarding those on Irish history, which were present in the 1960s; and even the argument about gender wasn't invented in the 1970s and 1980s. However, credit where credit is due – the emphasis on the complexity of social consciousness is to be welcomed, and it is important to make and stress the point that working-class conservatism in the nineteenth century was neither deviant nor insignificant.

Weaknesses
Nevertheless the weaknesses of Joyce's approach are much more pronounced than its strengths. For a start the style and tone is arrogant and pretentious. Rather than arguing Joyce pronounces and dismisses and appears to believe that more traditional forms of labour history have become moribund.

Neville Kirk pointed out that it is nonsensical to imagine that prior to Joyce and Stedman Jones all nineteenth century working-class experience was examined historically only in terms of class relations, but that does not mean that Chartism wasn't in fact a class-conscious movement. Lots of good work, not all by any means from Marxists, has appeared demonstrating the class-conscious nature of the Chartists' political outlook – for example by R A Sykes. All this is ignored by Joyce, as indeed he ignores the phenomenon of the cooperative movement in his argument regarding paternalism. In fact Joyce's definition of class is far too narrowly economic and economistic.

Instead it is necessary to contextualise the languages of the people and to consider *contested* meanings. Patrick Joyce doesn't do that. He takes language at face value and doesn't look at it politically. Insufficient attention is given to the concrete social situations in which discourse operates. The approach is empirically shallow and the ostensible meaning of political language is not deconstructed. In fact, what Joyce does is to reproduce the key tenets of bourgeois liberalism and say that they are true – insofar as a postmodernist can admit the existence of any truth. What we get is a whiggish version of ninteenth century history – 'the forward march of liberalism and the liberal people'. There is a political as well as an academic agenda present here.

Neville Kirk concluded with some further observations on Joyce's epistemology. His later work represents a descent into free-floating subjectivity and identity. It is perhaps not too surprising in those circumstances that he is turning increasingly towards biography. For example he takes John Bright at face value as a kind of saint in politics – with no reference to Bright's workplace tyranny. Economic and social issues are shunted to one side. The rules of historical method are thrown out of the window. Joyce's writings never mention ideology, but his work is profoundly ideological.

Alex Callinicos on Postmodernism

Alex Callinicos presented the final paper, which was focused upon postmodernism as a general concept. He opened by remarking that he viewed postmodernism as a sort of intellectual disease – or perhaps computer virus – which invades intellectual disciplines and reduces them to gibberish.

One force behind this trend, he argued, is the decline of the academic left. The impetus of the 1960s and 1970s has worked itself out and Marxists in the academy have been forced on to the defensive. Different aspects of postmodernism have significance for particular disciplines; in relation to history it has been characterised by a current in the philosophy of history which he characterised as 'narrativism', and which has its fountainhead in the work by Hayden White, *Metahistory*, which argued that the central concern of historiography was the historian's mode of emplotment. Contemporary forms of historical relativism are different from the old in that they focus not upon the subjectivity of the historian – cf. Collingwood – but the metaphysics of historical discourse. Foucault of course is a particularly important name in this connection.

According to Alex Callinicos, the effects of the trend are:

1. Hostility to any kind of theorising about history. He cited Lyotard in particular at this point, whose *The Postmodern Condition* had opened the attack on 'grand narratives', these of course being associated with the Enlightenment through to Hegel and Marx. The postmodern critique of 'grand narrative' converges with the

empiricists' distaste for theories of history in general and Marxism in particular.
2. Attacks on class analysis. Patrick Joyce's reader on 'Class', to take a particular example, is loaded down with impressionistic texts by poststructuralists.
3. Effacement of the distinction between history and fiction. The forms of historiography are alleged to be drawn from poetics and rhetoric. One can be dismissive regarding such uncontrolled experiments as Simon Schama's *Dead Certainties*, but this posture has sinister political implications – for example it suggests that the there is no way of achieving certainty about the truth of the Holocaust. Hayden White ties himself in knots because his philosophical position doesn't let him effectively confront the 'Holocaust revisionists'.

Alex Callinicos went on to ask how Marxists should respond. Certainly, a conception of language is crucial for one's conception of historical enquiry. Marx, in *The German Ideology*, gives attention to language and notes its constitutive character. Wittgenstein has demonstrated that language is *necessarily* a public and social practice. The first part of Patrick Joyce's or Gareth Stedman Jones' argument therefore isn't news, but what they do is to take it to unsustainable lengths with additional relativising steps. Their problem is that they rely on de Saussure's philosophy of language and fall into a form of idealism defined as 'textualism'.

Language
Still on the question of language, he went on to draw the contrast with the theory of language advanced by the philosopher Gottlob Frege, which incorporates the concept of a 'referent' and can therefore, unlike the Saussurian philosophy, formulate 'causal theories of reference', or as Hilary Putnum expressed it more colloquially, 'it ain't in the head'. The social context of utterance inhabits utterance itself. Carlo Ginsburg, for example, – no Marxist – alive to the nuances of languages as any postmodernist treats the language of historical records as an 'open window'. Contemporary sceptics regard it as a wall which precludes any reference to reality. Perhaps a better image is that of a distorted glass. He cited as exemplary a phrase from E P Thompson, 'the close integration of texts and contexts'.

Theory
Postmodernist hostility to historical theory draws on a basic objection to totalisations. However, the frequently cited contention by postmodernists that theoretical totalisation leads directly to totalitarianism, is itself an unmistakable variety of grand narrative.

The notion 'theory of history' can have a number of differentiated meanings:

1. It can structure a general account of the nature of human society – for example the concept of 'mode of production' in its different varieties does this.
2. It can attempt to identify the mechanisms of historical transformation responsible for the change from one era to another, for example, social contradictions. Such theories need not necessarily be Marxist – Michael Mann is a celebrated theorist in this field whose inspiration derives ultimately from Max Weber. Mann does not accord central significance to the mode of production as Marxists do, but treats social contradictions as variant and contingent combinations.
3. Historical theory can, more ambitiously, attempt to identify a directionality in history via general patterns of historical development, which may be viewed as progressive, regressive or cyclical, depending on the viewpoint. Marxist theory sees a long-term progressive trend in the development of productive forces; Weberian a more sombre form of progress in the elaboration of modes of domination.

Theories of history, Alex Callinicos emphasised, are to be distinguished from philosophies of history, for they do not rely, unlike the latter, on *teleological* explanation – that is, the interpretation of historical development in terms of a predetermined outcome which is taken as giving purpose to the historical process. Hegel is possibly the most important exponent of that approach.

So far as historiography is concerned, Marxism doesn't privilege certain genres, but postmodernism does – for example, its claim that a postmodern stance is necessary for certain forms of micro-history to be practised, such as the exploration of the symbolic. Its claims have been denounced in the strongest terms by Ginsburg as allied to those of fascism and its pet philosopher, Gentile. The absurdity of postmodernism's pretensions in this area are illuminated from the circumstance that one of the maestros of micro-history, E P Thompson, was a passionate opponent of every postmodernist historiographical claim.

Both Marxist and Weberian approaches, Alex Callinicos concluded, try to clarify their conceptual apparatus in a way which postmodernists take for granted. The latter rely on an unarticulated and unexamined conception of totality. Marxists and Weberians put their cards upon the table. He finished by quoting the injunction of Frederic Jameson: 'Always Historicise!'

Discussion
In the discussion which followed, one speaker noted that in the postmodern universe of equivalent worldviews it would make equal sense for Yorkshire Water to solve its drought problems by praying to the rain gods as much as by repairing its pipes. Another observed that however abstract postmodernism might be as a theoretical approach, once its adherents had secured a significant number of academic positions it had acquired a material base.

At the end of the meeting John Saville announced that he would be stepping down after approximately a decade of organising the group. John Charlton is to be his successor.

WHAT WENT WRONG IN THE SOVIET UNION AND EASTERN EUROPE?

This was the title of a conference held in April at Glasgow Caledonian University, jointly sponsored by the Socialist History Society and the Social Sciences Department of Caledonian University. The venue was chosen deliberately to counter the metropolitan bias which organisations centred in London tend to fall into. Over sixty participants attended, fairly evenly distributed between those coming from Scotland and those from south of the border.

After the formal opening Monty Johnstone delivered the first main paper on the theme of the October Revolution, asking the question of whether it should be considered a putsch or a popular revolution. His conclusion is that the Bolshevik Revolution was indeed the expression of mass popular support for the Bolshevik slogans of 'Peace, Bread and Land', but he then went on to demonstrate the way in which over subsequent months that support eroded, so that in the elections to the Constituent Assembly early in the following year the Bolshevik delegates and their allies were a minority, albeit still a very substantial one. The decision of Lenin's government not to accept the electoral verdict but instead to dissolve the Constituent Assembly by force was the point at which the new regime committed itself to pursuing what it regarded as historical necessity, even if need be in the face of majority opposition.

The second main session was opened by Professor R W Davies, who spoke on the theme of 'Stalinism' and in particular new evaluations and information which have emerged since the Soviet collapse and the significant – although still only partial – opening of the relevant archives. We now have valuable new insights on how the regime established itself and developed, although not sensationally new interpretations of its character.

The conference continued with four workshops, each one dealing with different episodes during which attempts were made at bringing about fundamental reforms in the USSR and the Soviet bloc. Dennis Ogden introduced a discussion on the USSR under Khrushchev; Martin Myant on the Prague Spring; Professor Stephen White, the leading authority on the Gorbachev years, opened on that theme; and Dr Andre Brie, of the PDS, who visited Glasgow especially for the conference, conducted a workshop on the end of the GDR and the reunification of Germany.

The closing plenary was held on Sunday morning, with Robin Blackburn's reflections on 'actually existing socialism' and its historical significance. It was an address which the participants found stimulating and thoughtful, not least in its questioning of certain concepts hitherto central to Marxist analysis.

It is hoped in due course to compile a volume containing the proceedings of the conference – readers will be kept informed.

LESLIE MORTON MEMORIAL LECTURE – SEPTEMBER 1995

Every available seat at Marx House was occupied on 16 September when Professor Paul Preston, the renowned biographer of Franco, delivered the Leslie Morton Memorial Lecture on the theme 'The Labour Government and Franco Fascism'.

It was a depressing story he had to relate. When the war ended there existed a general presumption that once the main fascist trunk had been cut down the Spanish branch, with its notorious friendly neutrality towards Hitler during the conflict, would not be able to survive very much longer. The election of a Labour government in Britain under a premier who had a unit of the International Brigades named after him, gave every reason for confidence in these hopes.

Tory agendas
Unhappily, in Spanish affairs as in much else, the new government soon picked up the agendas of previous Tory administrations. To conciliate the left a great deal of rhetorical condemnation was directed against the Franco regime, but the Foreign Office under Ernest Bevin systematically blocked any material initiatives which might have had a chance of undermining it. It was repeatedly asserted that it was the responsibility of the Spanish people themselves to deal with their tyrants, which, it was implied, they would soon do. This however was no more than a piece of cynical deception, in view of the decimation and prostration of the democratic forces in Spain and the regime's iron grip.

The US government was behaving in a similar fashion. President Truman genuinely hated and despised Franco, but deferred to his service chiefs who saw advantages in cooperating with the dictator. The ostensible international hostility without anything concrete being done to back it up gave Franco the best of both worlds. He was in no danger, but could present his regime to his adherents as besieged but continuing to fight a successful crusade against international freemasonry, the other face of Bolshevism.

Rehabilitation
With the onset of the Cold War a steady rehabilitation of Franco and his regime was conducted both in Britain and the US. His pro-Axis statements were increasingly expunged from the record and he was even presented in a contrary light, being referred to by his public relations spin-doctors as the allies 'silent ally' during the war. Following the Korean War the process was complete, and the regime, though remaining too obnoxious to gain formal admission into NATO, was fully integrated into the Western military framework, with US nuclear bases on its territory. Anglo-American anti-communism prolonged its life for thirty years beyond the point when it ought to have died and was universally expected to do so.

SOCIALIST HISTORY SOCIETY

Programme of Meetings 1996
Theme – 'Aspects of the Cold War'

20 January
    Soviet Foreign Policy – Dennis Ogden

23 March
    Branch Life in the CPGB in the Cold War –
    Renata Ahmed, Tony Dennis, Steve Woodhams

25 May
    Cold War in the Mediterranean – John Saville

13 July
    The Peace Movement in the Cold War – Bill Moore

21 SEPTEMBER

**A L MORTON MEMORIAL LECTURE:
THE COLD WAR AND THE LABOUR LEFT –
TONY BENN MP**
Lecture Theatre No. 1, University of Westminster,
Marylebone Road

16 November
    US Foreign Policy in the Cold War – Fred Halliday

All commence at 2.30 p.m. Lectures take place at Marx House, Clerkenwell Green, apart from the A L Morton Memorial Lecture on 21 September.

BACK ISSUES

Our History
(at 75p each)
58   Miners of Kilsyth in the 1926 General Strike: P&C Carter
65   The General Strike in Lanarkshire: John McLean
67   Spain against Fascism: Nan Green & AM Elliott
69   Rank and File Movements in Building, 1910–1920: P Latham
70   The Struggle against War and Facism, 1930–1939: Mike Power
71   From Radicalism to Socialism, Paisley Engineers 1890–1920: J Brown
72   People's Theatre in Bristol, 1930–1945: Angela Tuckett
73   TA Jackson – Centenary Appreciation: V Morton & S McIntyre
75   The 1842 General Strike in South Wales: Heather Jordan
76   Armed Resistance and Insurrection – early Chartist experience: John Baxter
77   Appeasement: Bill Moore
78   The Making of a Clydeside Working Class: Calum Campbell

(at £2.50 each)
79   1688 – How Glorious was the Revolution?: AL Morton
80   London Squatters 1946: ed Noreen Branson
81   The Anti-Fascist People's Front in the Armed Forces 1939–1946: eds. Bill Moore & George Barnsby
82   Labour–Communist Relations, Part 1, 1920–1935: eds. Noreen Branson & B Moore
83   Labour–Communist Relations, Part 2, 1935–1945: eds. Noreen Branson & B Moore
84/5 Labour–Communist Relations, Part 3, 1945–1951: B Moore
86   Power and Jurisdiction in Medieval England: R Hilton
87   Trotsky Reassessed: M Johnstone
88   1956 and the CPGB (Papers from a conference on this theme)

Our History Journal Nos 1–17   50p each
No 18 onwards   £2.50 each

Also available at £5.00 each plus 60p P&P
1939: The Communist Party and the War. eds. J Attfield & S Williams

OCCASIONAL PAPERS
No. 1
Jean Jones – *Ben Bradley Fighter for India's Freedom* – £2.50
No. 2
George Rudé 1910–1933 – Marxist Historian – Memorial Tributes – £2.50

Order from: The Secretary, Socialist History Society, 6 Cynthia Street, London N1 9JF

INDEX

adult education 23–46, 52, 62, 64, 70
Against University Standards (E P Thompson) 35, 36
Age of Extremes (Hobsbawm) 11, 54, 55, 59, 88
Alexander, Sally 94–6
Attlee, Clement 33, 40, 82, 83

'Battle of Ideas' 23, 37, 40
Bolsheviks 13, 14, 15, 16, 18, 83, 85, 88, 89, 122, 124
Border Country (Williams) 62, 65, 66, 67
Britain 62, 64, 65, 67, 74, 75, 79, 84, 91, 99, 103, 124
British Socialist Party (BSP) 81
Bukharin, Nikolai 85–6
Burnett, John 107
Burns, Emile 30, 39, 40

Callinicos, Alex 119–22
Chartism 114, 115, 116, 117, 118
Cold War, the 9, 19, 23, 30, 31, 33, 36, 39, 40, 42, 46, 61, 72, 77, 81, 124
communism 19, 30, 32, 33, 37, 39, 46, 55, 56, 57, 77, 82, 84, 85, 87, 89, 92, 93, 94
Communist International, the (Comintern) 13, 14, 15, 17, 18, 19, 81, 83, 84, 85, 86, 92, 98
Communist Party, the 8, 10, 13, 16, 17, 19, 20, 22, 28, 30–3, 37, 39, 40, 46, 61, 72, 77, 81–6, 106
Central Committee 18, 82
Cultural Committee 30–2, 39
Historians' Group 8–11, 51–2, 77
Writers' Group 30, 61
Culture and Society (Williams) 10, 62, 63, 64, 70

Davies, R W 123
de Saussure, Ferdinand 120
Deutscher, Isaac 9, 10

Dobb, Maurice 8, 10
Dutt, Rajani Palme 14, 15, 17, 20, 80, 83–5, 86

Eldridge, John and Lizzie 62–9
Eliot, T S 29, 30, 33, 38, 40, 43
'Emilism' 39, 40, 42
Europe 19, 92, 99, 100

feminist socialism 94–6
Fight for Manod, The (Williams) 62, 65, 67, 68
First World War 13, 81, 83, 100
Fourth International, the 87, 90

Germany 16, 55, 81, 82, 99, 103–5
Gorbachev, Mikhail 20, 86, 87, 123
Gorman, John 106–7
Graham, Desmond 98–101
Gramsci, Antonio 8, 15, 39, 91–4

Harrison, John 106
Hedeler, Vladislaw 85, 86
Hegel, Georg 119, 121
Heinemann, Margot 39, 77–8
Hill, Christopher 10, 52, 77
Hillenbrand, F K M 103–5
Hitler, Adolf 55, 81, 82, 104, 124
Hobsbawm, Eric 9, 10, 11, 52, 54–60, 61, 77, 88

Joyce, Patrick 116–19, 120

Kettle, Arnold 28, 33
Kiernan, Victor 10, 77, 107
Kirk, Neville 116–19
Khrushchev, Nikita 9, 13, 20, 82, 84, 123

Labour movement 61, 64, 75, 106
Labour Party 8, 16, 18, 71, 81, 82, 83, 84, 106, 117, 123, 124
Lenin, Vladimir Ilyich 13, 14, 15, 16, 17, 18, 83, 84, 123
Lindsay, Jack 30, 31, 32, 39

Long Revolution, The (Williams) 10, 62, 64
Loyalties (Williams) 63, 65, 67, 68
Lukacs, Gyorgy 14, 39

MacCarthy, Fiona 78–80
Making of the English Working Class, The (E P Thompson) 24, 44
Malthus, Thomas 114
Mandel, Ernest 87–90
Marx, Karl 6, 7, 52, 58, 119
Marxism 7, 8, 10–15, 32, 38, 39, 40, 52, 57, 58, 75, 77, 79, 85, 87, 88, 92, 118–23
McGrath, Tom 31, 44, 52
Morgan, Kevin 80, 82, 83
Morris, William 26, 28, 29, 323, 52, 78–80
Morton, A L 8, 10, 33, 77, 123

Owen, Robert 114

Palmer, Bryan 49–52
'PBEA' 35, 37, 44
Pollitt, Harry 14, 16, 17, 20, 33, 80–2, 86
postmodernism 116, 119–22

Raybould, Sidney 34, 35
Raymond Williams: Making Connections (Eldridge and Eldridge) 61–6, 68–9, 71–2
Rickword, Edgell 30, 39
Rothwell, Jerry 97
Rudé, George 10, 51
Russia 8, 9, 14, 16, 17, 18, 19, 20, 22, 39, 55, 56, 57, 62, 79, 81, 82, 83, 84, 85, 86, 88, 89, 90, 94, 98, 122, 123
Russian Revolution, the 9, 13, 14, 55, 81, 85, 87, 122

Samuel, Raphael 74–6
Saville, John 9, 10, 52, 113–16, 122

Second Generation (Williams) 62, 66, 67
Second World War 19, 55, 56, 59, 98–100, 103–5
socialism 3, 13, 22, 32, 38, 51, 61, 71, 72, 76–9, 87, 88, 90, 106
Stalin, Joseph 8, 9, 13, 18, 19, 20, 40, 55, 56, 79, 81, 84, 85, 87, 88, 93
Stalinism 8, 10, 11, 13, 18, 19, 20, 22, 23, 42, 88, 90, 123
Stedman Jones, Gareth 113–16, 117, 118, 120
Swingler, Randall 30, 31, 39, 40

Tebbutt, Melanie 101
Third International, the 14, 93
'Third Period', the 39, 86
Thompson, Dorothy 10, 49, 51, 52
Thompson, E P 10, 11, 22–46, 49–53, 78, 80, 120, 121
Thomson, George 30, 39
Tito, Marshal 19, 90
Torr, Dona 8, 33
Trotsky, Leon 8, 9, 15, 17, 87–90
Twentieth Congress, the 13, 20, 22

United States, the 50, 52, 56, 59, 76, 82, 99, 100, 118, 124

Volunteers, The (Williams) 63, 65, 67, 68
von Ranke, Leopold 67

Weber, Max 121, 122
West, Alick 33, 39
White, Haydn 119, 120
William Morris: Romantic to Revolutionary (E P Thompson) 32, 40
Williams, Raymond 10, 11, 61–72
Workers' Educational Association (WEA) 24, 33, 35, 37, 41, 44

Zhdanov, A A 9, 39